ENDORSEMENTS

Teachers in our Lutheran schools are stretched in many different directions. They are faced with unique situations and opportunities in which their values, beliefs, and constructs are challenged. *Prep Talks* tackles some of these situations through well-written and thought-provoking case studies. The various case studies presented in the book will spark deep conversations among professionals who strive to provide a Christ-based education to an ever-changing world. *Prep Talks* should be required reading not only for Lutheran Christian educators of all experience levels, but also for pastors, board members, and others involved in our Lutheran schools.

Dr. Chris Cody
Education Executive
South Wisconsin District, The Lutheran Church—Missouri Synod

Prep Talks is full of applicable situations that educators of all experience levels have or may face in the teaching profession. Readers will be challenged with struggles that affect the classroom that occur in the home, church, school, and community. Hearts will be stirred and thoughts provoked as readers wrestle with how best to analyze the situation, determine the best course of action, and finally implement plans for positive endings. *Prep Talks* is a great resource for staff development—especially for those who want to prepare for the unanticipated before it happens.

Michael Yurk
Principal
St. Paul Lutheran School, Grafton, WI

I absorbed *Prep Talks* in just three sittings. But it's too good for that! Savor it, suffer it, celebrate it in faculty and student discussions. It touches the challenging realities of teaching in Christian schools and covers a lifetime ministry of teaching experiences in one thought-provoking book. Thank God for the creative and deep-thinking insights and engagement of teachers Pingel, Bull, and Uden.

Edward Grube, LLD
Director of Publications and Communications
Lutheran Education Association

Prep Talks addresses many of the challenges and opportunities facing the educators working with students and families in our Lutheran schools. But instead of hitting you with heavy content, the short, entertaining stories disarm you as a reader and allow you to be honest in how your ministry wrestles with these issues. I enjoyed the questions at the end of each chapter as they would help to facilitate a great discussion among colleagues. I'm hoping one of our Michigan Lutheran schools invites me to a staff meeting for one of those discussions!

Travis Grulke
Assistant to the President—Superintendent of Schools
Michigan District, LCMS

PREP TALKS

TALES OF CHALLENGES & OPPORTUNITIES IN CHRISTIAN EDUCATION

BERNARD BULL · JIM PINGEL · MICHAEL UDEN

CONCORDIA PUBLISHING HOUSE · SAINT LOUIS

This is a work of fiction. Names, characters, businesses, places, events, locales, and incidents are either the products of the author's imagination or used in a fictitious manner. Any resemblance to actual persons, living or dead, or actual events is purely coincidental.

Founded in 1869 as the publishing arm of The Lutheran Church—Missouri Synod, Concordia Publishing House gives all glory to God for the blessing of 150 years of opportunities to provide resources that are faithful to the Holy Scriptures and the Lutheran Confessions.

3558 S. Jefferson Ave., St. Louis, MO 63118-3968
1-800-325-3040 • www.cph.org

Manufactured in the United States of America

Library of Congress Cataloging-in-Publication Data

Names: Bull, Bernard Dean, author. | Pingel, Jim, author. | Uden, Michael (Michael D.), author.
Title: Prep talks : tales of challenges & opportunities in Christian education / Dr. Bernard Bull, Dr. James Pingel, and Dr. Michael Uden.
Description: St. Louis, MO : Concordia Publishing House, [2019] | Includes bibliographical references and index.
Identifiers: LCCN 2019002353 (print) | LCCN 2019011856 (ebook) | ISBN 9780758659323 | ISBN 9780758659316 (alk. paper)
Subjects: LCSH: Church schools--United States. | Christian education--United States.
Classification: LCC LC368 (ebook) | LCC LC368 .B85 2019 (print) | DDC 371.071--dc23

LC record available at https://lccn.loc.gov/2019002353

1 2 3 4 5 6 7 8 9 10 28 27 26 25 24 23 22 21 20 19

DEDICATION

Dedicated to mission-minded risk-takers, dreamers, and difference-makers who persistently join in co-creating the future of Lutheran education.

—Bernard Bull

Dedicated to those inspired and called to minister according to the Way, God's truth, and Jesus' life.

—Jim Pingel

Dedicated to the preservice teachers with and from whom I have learned in the School of Education at Concordia University Wisconsin since 1998. By now, many are veteran educators themselves, but their love for learning, students, and our Savior inspires and encourages me still.

—Michael Uden

ACKNOWLEDGMENTS

I am grateful for the many teachers who contributed to my own formation as an educator; for my family, for not only enduring but also embracing the seemingly constant twists and turns of my life and work; and for Dr. William Cario, who supported and encouraged my leadership, scholarship, and writing for almost thirty years.

—Bernard Bull

I want to thank my former colleagues and friends at Sheboygan Lutheran High School (Sheboygan, WI) and Mayer Lutheran High School (Mayer, MN)—individuals who faithfully served in the trenches with me and who shaped my Christian leadership walk for life. I think of them, and the real-life ministry experiences we endured, learned from, and celebrated, almost every day.

—Jim Pingel

I am blessed beyond measure by God's gift of my family: my wife, children, and grandchildren. You know me fully, encourage and inspire me daily, and love me still. I also gratefully acknowledge the children from foster care whose lives and stories I have studied, shaped, and shared. Your courage, vulnerability, and resiliency are gifts I hold close.

—Michael Uden

TABLE OF CONTENTS

INTRODUCTION

Fictional Stories with Real-World Implications

BY BERNARD BULL

"If these walls could talk." Every Christian classroom is the set and stage for dozens, hundreds, even thousands of stories. These stories represent the countless moments, challenges, and joys of Christian education. They are stories about teachers and their journey to help students develop in mind, body, and spirit. They are stories of students and all that they bring with them to the classroom. They are stories of faith and doubt, victory and disappointment, judgment and forgiveness, change and constancy, wonder and boredom, community and isolation, tradition and innovation, conflict and resolution, pain and comfort, learning and unlearning, clarity and confusion, Law and Gospel. Within these stories are rich lessons about the past and present as well as sources of wisdom for the future.

Ask any student or teacher who has spent more than a few months in a classroom, and they will surely have many stories to tell. Yet, while the actual stories of the classroom are quite powerful and can often be shared, sometimes they are too close, too personal, and too private. They are better left untold, or at least revised to respect and protect the people involved. At the same time, they are too important to be left untold. They contain too much wisdom to be squandered. How do we share these stories?

This book is one possibility. In the following twenty chapters, some more in depth, others only a few short pages, you will find stories of the modern Christian classroom and school. None of them are true stories in the sense that they actually happened at a particular time or in a particular place. Yet each one of them is drawn from the realities of modern education. They reflect some of the pressing questions, increasingly common challenges, and any number of important themes in Christian education today.

In some cases, a chapter is a compilation of many stories. In other instances, it is inspired by an actual event. Yet they are all ultimately stories, what you might consider fictional case studies, intended to serve as a way to help you reflect on the realities of the Christian school in a contemporary age. They invite you to consider the challenges, questions, and realities of actual teachers and students. Some read as incredibly realistic, so much so that many readers will relate with all or part of a story. "That story is my story," some might feel. Others are more fantastical, even verging on hyperbole or what one might consider a Disney version of the real thing. The beginning and ending might be a bit too clean and too simple for you. No worries. After all, they are ultimately stories.

In fact, that is one of the benefits of using fictional case studies to reflect and further prepare for life in the modern Christian school. They are separated just enough from the real world to give you greater opportunity to critique them with abandon. You can take what is useful and leave what is not. You can challenge some of them as unrealistic while embracing others as inspiration to create similar, real-life versions of the story in your own classroom or school.

Fictional case studies might not recall real events, but they can offer real and important insights. They can invite us to imagine, to reflect, and to discuss, and that is one of the prime purposes of this book. While you are certainly free to read this book alone, we designed it to be consumed in community, as fuel for the fire of discussion among classroom teachers and administrators. Our hope is that this book will serve as the spark for countless hours of discussion and even more reflection. May it aid you as you grapple with what it means to be faithful to God's call in Christian education, as well as consider some of the distinctive features of Christian education in this particular age.

These are far from an exhaustive or even a systematic collection of stories. In fact, we made no effort even to arrange the stories by a given theme, nor did we strive to cover a specific list of critical issues. This loose structure gives you an extra measure of freedom to read the chapters in whatever order you deem most useful. Skip to the chapters that capture your interest or are most relevant to your current situation. Return to others when they are most appropriate.

There are so many other important stories to be told, and we hope that this book might even inspire others to join in the story creation and storytelling. What these stories all represent are challenges and questions of this age. They are an invitation to pray, discuss, and consider the implications for your context, to read them and seek out wisdom from God's Word as you ponder their relevance for your important work.

Some topics are far more intense and emotionally laden than others. You will find fictional cases about loss, fear, and trauma. At the same time, you will find other stories that venture into what seem like the more mundane aspects of a modern school, such as awards banquets and grading systems. However, every story includes one or more moments of tension and conflict. They are intended to draw you and others into personal and group consideration about how we might respond, prepare for, or learn from them. They will invite you to think about the lives and backgrounds of students, the formation of one's personal philosophy of education, and what it means truly to live out the mission, vision, values, and goals of a distinctly Christian school.

As the owner of this book, you are free to use it as you wish, but I'm compelled to share what I hope will happen. What I imagine is a group of teachers, perhaps a small group of friends who all teach, or maybe a faculty gathering for weekly meetings. I picture them reading one of the shorter or longer case studies in advance and then gathering to use that case study as a launchpad into a rich and vibrant discussion. Some will be inspired by what they read. Others will be troubled or even annoyed.

The questions at the end of the chapter will offer a starting point, and people will begin to share their real-world stories and examples. They will discuss and maybe even debate some of the themes and ideas. They will turn to the Scriptures for wisdom amid this discussion. Some in the discussion will be inspired to explore further or even to consider changes to their classroom. Perhaps a small group will gather in a follow-up meeting to consider next steps. Yet before any of that happens, the entire group will come together in prayer, asking for God's wisdom and grace as they venture into their respective classrooms, participating in creating many more real and important stories of Christian education. It is with this hope that I am honored that you've elected to open this book, to read it, and to use it as a resource as you strive to grow as a Christian educator.

DREAMS AND MUSINGS OF A MODEL STUDENT AND AN ASPIRING TEACHER

BY BERNARD BULL

Candice couldn't wait to begin her calling as a teacher. With fond memories of her childhood schools and teachers, her own experience as a middle school student shaped her dreams and expectations of that future classroom where she would stand in front of the class, smiling but firm, and the students would sit attentively, anxious to learn. Of course, that is not exactly what happened in her childhood classrooms, but Candice was a model student, an excellent and obedient pupil throughout her years in elementary and high school. She loved the order and structure of school. She got it. She had high marks. She tested well. Her color-coded binders never lacked order. Even her penmanship rivaled the precision of what you might find in a typed and printed essay.

Candice received countless accolades and affirmations when she was a student, which only further served to solidify her love for the classroom and fuel her desire to become a teacher one day. While she would not necessarily explicitly state as much, Candice loved the way that many of her teachers commanded the classroom and seemed to have the respect and admiration of students, parents, and others in the community. She admiringly recounted the stack of cards and small thank-you gifts that filled the desks of some of her most beloved teachers during the Christmas season.

She was not unaware of some of the challenges associated with teaching. Salaries varied widely from one school to the next. There seemed to be a growing dissatisfaction with schools in the media. The respect for teachers ebbed and flowed, especially outside of the school walls. In addition, she realized that external mandates and growing interests in high-stakes testing put some limits on teachers that could be problematic. Despite these and related challenges, as Candice diligently worked her way through a college teacher education program, she still wanted to be a teacher. She wanted to shape young minds, help students grow and develop, nurture their faith, and work right in the heart of a Christian education system that had served her so well, one that encouraged and affirmed her daily.

Every day, this young woman dreamed of that day when she would be a teacher and have her own classroom. She imagined how she would decorate the room. She thought of how she would plan that first day of class. Whenever she learned something new, Candice soon found herself pondering how to teach the content or concept to her future students in a fun and memorable way. Candice had a keen and unusual focus on becoming a teacher, so much so that she sought out countless volunteer teaching opportunities even as she finished her studies in both high school and college.

When Candice graduated from high school, she spent the summer working at a STEM camp and doing volunteer work for a couple other education-related events in her community. From there, she moved across the country to one of the top-ranked Christian teacher education programs in the nation. She entered college with the same confidence that served her so well in high school, and it worked.

Then came the day for her very first teacher education class, a course that served as a foundation and introduction to the teaching profession. She got to class early, had her laptop fully charged and ready, and took her place in the second row of the class (she didn't want to come off as too enthusiastic). Professor Janice Edwards entered the room, turned to the class, and proceeded to ask a series of questions that would start Candice on a new journey in her preparation for teaching.

- What is the ultimate purpose of school?
- What is the difference between school and education?
- What are the absolutely essential elements of a great education—and don't let any non-essentials creep into your answers?
- Whom do schools serve the best? Whom do they fail to serve well? Why?
- What policies and practices in schools are getting in the way of helping the greatest number of people reach the highest levels of learning?
- What role should curiosity and a love of learning play in school?

It was a three-hour night class, and after each of these questions, the professor stayed silent until two or three students responded to each. Deeply curious about every response, Professor Edwards asked follow-up questions or invited others to build upon or challenge the previous comments. After three hours of this dialogue, Candice was exhausted from the depth of the conversation. She'd never experienced something like this before. She also found herself with an uncomfortable and uncommon experience: self-doubt.

Candice had dreamed of being a teacher since as far back as she could remember, and not once had she asked herself any of these questions. She never thought about the ultimate purpose of school, what was essential for great learning, how school hurts or helps learning, or even the role of curiosity and a love of learning in a school context. She loved learning, but she mostly did work in school to get a good grade, to open the next door of opportunity, and to receive the praise and encouragement that comes from a job well done. Even after others left the room, Candice sat there pondering. How could she have gone this far without asking such fundamental questions about an education system that occupied over twenty-five thousand hours of her life up to that point?

She found herself experiencing what some might describe as a sort of existential crisis, at least with regard to her longtime aspiration to become a teacher. Becoming a teacher is not enough. In fact, the more Candice thought about it, the more she became convinced that she needed to stop thinking about becoming a teacher and instead start thinking about how she could become a champion for a rich, meaningful, deep, and impactful learning experience for as many people as possible. It was not about being a teacher. This single conversation led her to have a new mission that had less to do with her and some preconceived notion of what it means and looks like to be a professional educator. Candice's new mission focused on learners, not on teachers or even on becoming one.

She pondered this new perspective most of the night and woke up early for a jog around campus. As she was running, she saw her professor walking into one of the buildings. Candice was not an especially bold or outgoing person, but after mulling over this issue for almost twelve hours straight, all of it largely sparked by that professor the day before, she could have few inhibitions. She ran over to Professor Edwards, shouting her name even as she was still twenty or thirty yards away. She was a bit startled, but she turned in Candice's direction and waited for her to get closer. She recognized her from class and even remembered her name.

In a frenzy of semi-coherent statements, Candice proceeded to tell the professor her story. She explained how she had wanted to be a teacher since childhood. She talked about the role of school in her life. She also explained the torment and confusion of the past twelve hours, wondering how she could be such a successful student in this system for so many years, aspire to be a teacher for over a decade, and never consider any of the questions posed by the professor the day before.

Then she simply asked her for help. “Now what do I do? Where do I go from here?”

The professor commended her for the struggle and said, “Those seem like very important questions to you. What will you do with them? Do you have any ideas on how you want to go about answering them?” Initially annoyed at not getting a direct answer and resolution to her dilemma, she realized that the professor had no intention of giving her an answer or solving this problem for her. She offered no answers, only questions that somehow helped her clarify her thinking and pursue answers to her own questions. At the same time, she felt heard and honored. It was as if Professor Edwards believed in Candice’s ability to find such answers, that she was genuinely interested in her learning journey, but that she saw it as entirely her own learning journey and responsibility.

This, too, was a brand-new experience for Candice. Some past teachers had asked questions, but they usually seemed to have a set answer in mind. All she had to do was get to the right answer and then bask in the smile and admiration that she received when she got it right. Professor Edwards approached the conversation differently. She didn’t seem to have a definitive answer in mind. She was more curious about where Candice would take all of this.

As Candice talked with the professor, a plan started to emerge. “I think that I want to find out how other people answer the questions you posed in class yesterday. I want to find out how people’s answers to these questions impact how different schools work and how students go about learning. I want to discover the role of both teachers and students in different schools. Maybe I can interview school leaders, teachers, and students. I can observe them and see where things go from there.” She saw a familiar look on her professor’s face. It was a look of approval and encouragement, but something about it seemed different than what she experienced in the past, even though she couldn’t put it into words.

"That sounds like a fascinating project, Candice. Would you consider keeping me posted about what you find out? Maybe you could share your research with the class at some point."

For the next four months, Candice interviewed over thirty people and visited eighteen different schools. She went to urban, suburban, and rural schools. She went to public, public charter, independent, and faith-based schools. She went to traditional community schools, magnet schools, and experiential schools. She went to a Montessori school, a Waldorf school, a Sudbury school, a STEM academy, a school of the arts, a project-based-learning school, a bilingual school, a classical school, and even a virtual school. She interviewed leaders, teachers, and students from these and many other schools as well. She gathered pages of notes, questions, and observations. In every interview and every school visit, she framed her research around those initial questions posed by her professor along with some of her own: questions about the purpose of school, essential attributes, features that enhance and detract from learning, and much more. Candice observed the way in which teachers and students saw their roles in these schools. She learned about the consistency (or lack thereof) between what people said they believed about school and learning and what they actually practiced.

Finally, only a week before the end of the semester, Candice sat in her dorm room scanning pages and pages of notes. She looked at these artifacts from the largest project of her life. She experienced incredible pride and contentment with her work over the semester, a satisfaction very different from getting an A on a big test or project. She didn't do this for a teacher or a class. This project grew out of a driving question in her mind, a deep curiosity and sense of disequilibrium. She still didn't have all the answers, but she did have a much greater sense of the possibilities. Candice understood the nuances behind answers to many of her questions. She also saw a personal set of convictions begin to emerge in her own mind about schooling and her philosophy of education.

Drawing from her notes and reflections, Candice began preparation for her big presentation in class. She didn't have to give the presentation. She wanted to do it. She looked forward to taking people on a tour of her journey and how it transformed her from being an aspiring teacher to becoming an aspiring champion of a rich and diverse education system. Perhaps she would still become a teacher. Perhaps not. Either way, she would never be the same.

Reflection and Discussion

While Candice's level of focus and effort might seem extreme to many readers, it helps us highlight important questions about our own beliefs and values about education. The following questions give you an opportunity to step into Candice's shoes and consider some of your own ideas about education.

1. Candice had what seemed like an idyllic experience as a student, which in turn influenced her beliefs and aspirations about teaching. How did your experiences as a student influence what you believe and think about education?
2. For Candice, this first education class was a key turning point. Can you identity key events or lessons that shaped you as a Christian educator?
3. Revisit the list of questions posed by the professor in Candice's first education class. How would you answer each of those questions?
4. If someone asked you to describe your philosophy of education, what would you tell him or her?
5. How does a Christian worldview and Scripture inform your philosophy of education?
6. How much does your philosophy of education align with what you actually do in the classroom?

IT'S ALL ABOUT JESUS

Can a School Integrate Faith and Learning If Its Faculty Do Not?

BY MICHAEL UDEN

When Christ the Rock Christian School was established in 1984, neither Candace Christensen nor Nora Hargrove, two of its current teachers, had yet been born. Perhaps that is an important reminder of how God's work and plan far exceed the lifespan of any person.

The school was founded by a group of deeply devoted Christian families who wanted to provide a distinct option for their children as well as others who sought a school in which Christ was part of the entire curriculum, not just at morning prayer or closing devotion. The region surrounding the school had very few parochial school options at the time, and with the prayer and financial support of several nondenominational Christian churches at the onset, the new school quickly thrived. Within three years, it was serving more than two hundred children in kindergarten through eighth grade.

In its early years, the staff of Christ the Rock Christian School consisted primarily of members from its founding congregations. This resulted in a deeply committed Christian faculty, many of whose own children attended the school as well. The school's mission for full integration of faith and learning throughout every component of the day was palpable. On the rare occasion when additional staff was needed, a cadre of newly minted educators from Bible colleges was eager and ready to answer the call. Christ the Rock garnered a well-earned reputation for strong academics and equally strong faith integration.

By the time the school celebrated its twenty-fifth anniversary, few if any of the surnames from the charter roster could be found on its class lists, as those children had long since grown and pursued their lives elsewhere. The neighborhood surrounding Christ the Rock had also changed, mirroring the broader community the school attempted to serve. Manufacturing, once the backbone for employment in the area, was nearly extinct; more than a few of the houses tucked within the tree-lined streets in the blocks surrounding the school were vacant and in disrepair. Had it not been for the state voucher program that enabled low- and mid-income families to enroll in private and faith-based schools, Christ the Rock may not have survived the last decade. Buoyed by public funding, the school enrollment matched its early days; however, the population it served—as well as those serving—was very different than at the start.

No longer was it typical that a family at Christ the Rock be active within a Christian congregation. Instead, families chose Christ the Rock for its proximity or record of safety far more often than for its mission of integrating Christ in all things. The school faculty also ran the gamut of those having grown up in the Christian faith to those simply needing a job and being drawn to the smaller size and restrictions of a private school. Nora Hargrove began her career as a second-grade teacher at Christ the Rock directly upon graduation from a small Christian liberal arts college, where she majored in Christian elementary education. Her parents raised Nora and her siblings in the Church, and Nora herself had attended Christian schools her entire life. She was drawn to Christ the Rock because it matched her own experience so closely—and because second grade was the level she loved most.

Candace Christensen, her colleague and the third-grade teacher, had been teaching at Christ the Rock for four years, after an initial two-year professional stint in a large public school district. Candace accepted the job at Christ the Rock because she chaffed at the bureaucracy she experienced in the large public district and sought to be in a smaller school environment. Christ the Rock was an easy commute from her apartment, and she loved the third graders and the families she served. Unlike Ms. Hargrove, Ms. Christensen had always attended public schools and categorized herself "Christian friendly" more than Christian.

Nora felt a compelling call to share Christ with every student and family she met at school. She utilized a theme verse from Scripture each week of the year and incorporated it in her parent newsletter as well as in her daily lessons. Every lesson was a chance to point students to Christ and to highlight how Christ is in all things. Not only had this truth been emphasized throughout Nora's university training, but the perspective had also been instilled in her from the very beginning of her life. Her mother and father began and ended each day with reading and reflection from God's Word. As a result, Nora had biblical connections for every subject and was happiest when she could communicate the Christian curricular ties.

These opportunities did not bring Candace the same joy. Although she had been baptized as a toddler at the insistence of her great-grandmother, who died before Candace could inquire about the fuss, she did not grow up in the Church. The few experiences Candace had while attending Christian services struck her as superficial and forced. The pious in attendance did not acknowledge her, much less greet her; no one seemed better behaved or happier as a result of the time served. Moreover, Candace was sick of hearing about self-righteous religious leaders caught in yet another scandal. While she recognized there might be some legitimate Christ followers out there—she might cite Mother Teresa—Candace believed fervently that everyone should find their own path and be kind and decent to one another along the way. If pressed, she would acknowledge that she believed in some sort of higher power, but who, what, and why were yet to be determined fully.

Such contrasts occasionally caused some fissures among the faculty at Christ the Rock, and the school's administrator, Michelle Valdez-Pritching (or MVP, as she was affectionately known by both school faculty and families), did her best to hold things together. Mrs. Valdez-Pritching had been Christ the Rock's administrator for nearly ten years, and she knew well the demands of keeping a voucher school running and fully staffed.

MVP, a devout Catholic, screened every teacher applicant to discern his or her level of support for the school's Christian mission. While Candace may have given a stronger impression of her Christian affinity in her interview than what was true, she also came to the school with two years of experience and seemed unfazed by both the expectations of the job as well as the modest salary. As Michelle came to know each of her staff, she recognized clearly that some faculty members were more invested in the namesake of Christ the Rock than others, and she attempted to remedy that. Each Monday, she began the mandatory faculty meeting with a devotion and prayer. Each classroom was required to have Jesus Time as part of each day's schedule, and Michelle had engaged area pastors and parent volunteers during her first two summers at the school to review and revamp the entire Jesus Time curriculum, grades K through 8. As a result, every teacher now had a scripted curriculum for use during each of the 180 school days. The daily curriculum included a Scripture verse and discussion questions as well as a related keyword or concept that the teacher could integrate throughout the day if they chose.

For her part, Candace used the Jesus Time curriculum once or twice a week if her schedule allowed. Her real passion in instruction was language arts, and her third graders had standardized test scores to demonstrate that she was a most effective educator in this area. Her classroom climate was extremely welcoming, and her classroom management was highly engaging. For those reasons, Principal MVP was content to have an effective and committed teacher on her staff and took solace in considering that students had a significantly stronger Christian role model in both their second- and fourth-grade years.

Nora Hargrove incorporated Jesus Time each and every day in her classroom, but she also wanted deeply to serve within a faculty that sought to grow and encourage one another in their Christian faith as much as she did. When taking the job at Christ the Rock, she considered that she was stepping into a ministry. Michelle impressed that perspective on Nora in her interview, and early in her tenure several of her Christ the Rock colleagues invited Nora to join an after-school Bible study group, which met on Fridays. When the core leaders of the study group left Christ the Rock for retirement or a spouse's job promotion, Nora tried to keep the Friday afternoon fellowship alive. After three weeks of being the only one there, however, she gave up and focused fully on the spiritual development of her students instead. Without question, the Holy Spirit worked through her earnest efforts. Ms. Hargrove delighted in three pictures displayed on the edge of her desk, each one portraying the Baptism of various former students she had served within her class.

When Candace Christensen was hired, Nora Hargrove was ecstatic to welcome her to the community of Christ the Rock Christian School, primarily because she was the only other teacher in her twenties, and she would also be receiving Nora's second-grade graduates in the fall. The two had much in common when it came to navigating the process for obtaining state licensure as out-of-state applicants or sharing curricular best practices, and their initial lunch meetings were full of laughter and excitement. Early during that first fall term, which fell during a presidential election, Nora had been transparent with Candace regarding her pro-life stance and how it informed her voting choices. When Candace quickly changed the topic of conversation, Nora was caught off-guard, but not nearly as much as by Candace's new discussion: how she planned to welcome her boyfriend when he came home to their apartment that night after a week away for business. Instantly, Nora learned that Candace was living with her boyfriend in a decidedly non-platonic relationship, and she was crestfallen.

Although Nora offered virtually nothing in response to Candace's unwittingly candid conversation, Nora was far more engaged in the internal discussions she facilitated in her head in the days and weeks that followed. During these internal debates, Nora alternated between action plans: from a winsome consideration of how she might witness to Candace and encourage her to explore the specific what and why of Christianity more fully, to a legalized scheme designed to bring her colleague's moral shortcomings to the attention of their school administrator. She was also well aware of Candace's disdain for fallen leaders in the church, and Nora echoed the disdain and disappointment that Candace expressed each time. Yet Nora saw this as the conniving power of sin in a person's life rather than confirmation that Christianity—or, far more directly, the Christ of Christendom—was somehow implicated or discredited in the process.

Most of all, Nora was concerned about the impact of Candace's integration—or the more likely absence—of the Christian faith within her classroom. Occasionally, Nora would walk into Candace's room while she was teaching in order to drop off something or pass along a needed update. During such impromptu visits, Nora was often surprised and saddened by what she witnessed. For example, one day she entered the room and was encouraged to see Candace finishing what appeared to be that day's segment of Jesus Time. During her classroom entrance, Nora discerned that the text of the day was Jesus raising Lazarus from the dead, which she knew from memory to be John 11. Nora's initial encouragement quickly evaporated, however, when she heard Candace question, "Why do you think Lazarus was excited and hopeful to see Jesus when He came to visit?" Nora was then further disheartened, albeit slightly proud, to hear one of her second-grade graduates respond, "Ms. Christensen, I don't think Lazarus was excited when Jesus came to his house because he was dead then." As Nora reached Candace's podium to hand her the permission slips for the trip to the city museum that both classes had been planning, she caught a glimpse of the Jesus Time curriculum guide and that day's lesson heading, "Hope for Lazarus." Had her colleague even read the biblical text beforehand? Nora's heart and mind stirred in her a stew of frustration, dismay, and guilt as she closed the door and headed back to her classroom.

During the quarterly summative evaluation meeting with Principal MVP that winter, Nora bit her lip for a moment before beginning her response to the question, "What suggestions do you have that could help to improve the culture and community of Christ the Rock Christian School as a whole?" How might she share her concerns and observations without seeming like a busybody or a gossip? Might Mrs. Valdez-Pritching already know about them and be addressing them with Candace individually? As a Christian, Nora knew she should approach Candace as outlined in Matthew 18, but she most certainly did not know how. Would raising her fears and frustration with her principal now give her more direction regarding how to navigate this path, or would it cause her to lose the respect of her school leader and her professional foothold in the process?

"Michelle, I would like to know how you envision building and conveying a common set of beliefs and practices for faculty about Christ the Rock's expectations for a Christ-centered community," Nora began. "I think of Proverbs 27:17, 'Iron sharpens iron, and one man sharpens another.' I want to serve within a school ministry community in which we are all growing in our Christian faith and holding one another accountable, both for our actions at school as well as our lives outside of the school day. I think it would also improve the ministry we provide to our students and families."

"Thank you for raising the topic, Nora," Michelle responded. "As I think you know, I am very clear with anyone who steps into our building—prospective faculty, family, or student—that we are a Christian school. I also worked to develop a comprehensive curriculum for Jesus Time when I first came to Christ the Rock. Our staff handbook also provides guidelines for how faculty members are to conduct themselves in the classroom, including ideas for how to integrate the Christian faith."

"But what about requirements? What if your suggestions are not considered expectations?" Nora pleaded, realizing her emotion had risen to the surface in swift fashion.

"Just as I meet every student where they are, I try to do the same with the staff. Some people are more comfortable in sharing their Christian faith than others, and some teachers are also able to incorporate Christ into their teaching more easily. You have a great ability in that area, Nora." Michelle's compliment condemned more than affirmed Nora, who wrestled again with whether she should have first begun this critical conversation with her colleague Candace. Now she wondered how and when this unchartered conversation with her administrator might end.

"Thank you." Nora's upbeat expression belied her inner turmoil. "I guess I feel torn sometimes with my focus on our school's namesake—Christ the Rock—and how the Holy Spirit can work to build my life on that unshakable bedrock as well as how I might encourage those around me to do the same. At other times, I feel instead like I am holding a rock in my hand, like the Pharisees in John 8, and I am left convicted by Christ's words, 'Let him who is without sin among you be the first to throw a stone'" (John 8:7).

"I want to understand this conundrum, Nora." Michelle's tone was disarming and welcoming, and Nora was drawn to the compassion and sincerity she felt from MVP. "Please help me by giving me some examples."

Reflection and Discussion

Scripture provides many examples and directives regarding how we are to work as part of the kingdom of God. Read and reflect on the following Scripture passages as part of this chapter discussion: 1 Peter 3:15; Matthew 5:16; Colossians 4:2–6; 2 Timothy 2:15; 1 Peter 3:2.

1. Is mere respect or appreciation of a school's Christian mission sufficient for its faculty and staff? How important is it for every member of the professional team to practice a Christian faith inside and outside the school day?
2. Not every teacher has a parallel set of skills or confidence in teaching the Christian faith. How should a school and its leader address that?
3. Were the teaching and classroom interactions of a colleague's classroom any of Nora Hargrove's business? Should such matters only be the concern of the school administrator?
4. How should a Christian school best cultivate a Christian community of Law and Gospel for all whom it serves—including its faculty and staff members?

MIXED MESSAGES

Creation and Evolution

BY JIM PINGEL

THEOLOGY

As Mr. Simon Tolaez wrote the number 9 on the whiteboard, he asked his class, “So what does this symbol represent?” The eighth-grade students at St. Peter’s Lutheran School responded, almost in unison, “Nine!”

“That’s right,” Tolaez confirmed. “The number nine.” Then he added a number 1 next to the 9. “Now what do these numbers represent?”

“Ninety-one!” most in the class responded.

“Good,” Tolaez responded. “I always knew you were a bright group.” Then he added another 1 after the 91. “Now what do you see?”

A few eighth graders shouted out “nine hundred eleven.” Some others, though, paused. “That’s 9-1-1, the number you are supposed to dial for an emergency,” said one. Another student, who had a passion for history, chimed in with something different. “But what you have up there, Mr. Tolaez, could also be referring to the 9/11 attacks on the United States, with the planes flying into the World Trade Center and all that stuff.”

“So which is it, people?” Tolaez asked his students—loving the cognitive dissonance stirring in the brains of his young pupils. “Is it nine hundred eleven? Is it an emergency call? Or is it a historical reference to a national tragedy our country endured almost two decades ago? Who’s right?” Borrowing this introduction used by Dr. Del Tackett in

The Truth Project, Tolaez asked his students to conduct a think-pair-share for two minutes before one person in the grouping would share the pair's conclusions. As they spoke, most pairs concluded that the correct answer to the question depended on one's knowledge, experiences, and viewpoint or worldview.

In addition to the savvy hook Tolaez used to introduce the new unit on the worldview battle between creationism and evolution, he then shared a brief headline from a blog stating that archaeologists had recently discovered fossilized teeth of a great white shark in the rubble of South Dakota. Tolaez explained that an evolutionist might argue that billions and billions of years ago, when South Dakota was underwater, a shark died and its remains settled at the bottom of an ocean, where it became fossilized. On the other hand, a creationist might argue that the fossil finding provides hard evidence of a global flood as described in the Book of Genesis. The massive movement of sediment during the turbulent flood would certainly have buried so many different land and sea creatures. Tolaez made the point that the evidence—the teeth of a great white shark buried in the rock of South Dakota—remained indisputable in both worldviews. The dispute or debate is not over the evidence, however, but over the interpretation of the evidence.

In addition to being a Bible-believing creationist, Tolaez explained that he found the great flood explanation more compelling and believable from a scientific perspective anyway. What made more sense—that a shark died, settled to the bottom of an ocean, and slowly but surely accumulated sediment on top of it without any disturbances or current shifts on the ocean floor over billions of years? Or that a great flood moved sediment at such a rapid rate that it caught and buried many creatures in a moment of tectonic upheaval? He let his students ponder his essential worldview question without answering it himself. Next he showed numerous slides of fossils that depicted fish eating other fish, thus indicating that these sea creatures were buried in sediment instantaneously and not over billions and billions of years.

Enola Rettam listened with disdain to her theology teacher give his creationist account. Surely he realized how out of touch he sounded. Everyone knew the theory of evolution was factual. The fossil record proved it, and most scientists believed it; no, they *knew* that evolution explained the origin of the cosmos and humankind. When she heard Mr. Tolaez say that the earth was only thousands of years old, and not billions, she almost fell out of her chair. "Mr. Tolaez," she asked, "then how come most people and scientists think the earth is billions of years old?"

"Well, it goes back to the point we've been trying to make here all morning, Enola," he patiently responded. "People want to believe what confirms their own worldview or position. It's often called 'confirmation bias.' If you believe there is no God, then you have to explain things from that perspective. If you believe in God, then that gives you a lens to view the world through too." He saw Enola shaking her head and smirking.

"But science has proven that the world is billions and billions of years old," Enola argued. "Everyone knows this. Scientists and archaeologists keep finding more and more evidence to show that evolution is true. I mean, you do believe that things can change over time, don't you?"

"Yes, but this is where we need to define our terms," Tolaez explained as if he had been waiting for this question to be asked. "If you're talking about evolution as being about change—well of course I believe in change. I hope I can change my eating habits and lose twenty-five pounds this summer!" Some in the class laughed at their teacher, but not Enola. "But if we are talking about the theory of evolution, in terms of different species or kinds changing into other kinds—you know, cats becoming dogs, or amoebas becoming apes and then apes becoming humans—that is not something God's Word teaches and, quite frankly, is very unscientific too."

Rennis Demeeder, a pastor's kid sitting next to Enola, entered the conversation. "Well, let me ask you something, Enola. Where do you think all the stuff that makes up the universe came from in the first place?"

"It came from the big bang, or some kind of soup or lake full of matter and stuff," Enola replied. "Then it exploded and all of life was set in motion. That's why it took billions and billions of years to evolve to get to where things are at today," she explained, hesitating just a bit as she listened to her own words.

"But how did that 'matter and stuff,' way back before the big bang or whatever, get there?" Rennis wanted to know. Enola remained silent for a moment before responding.

"Well, I'm not sure, but I suppose you're going to tell me God created it. But where did God come from, then?"

"God has always been here, Enola, that's what I'm saying!" Rennis insisted.

"But you have no scientific proof of that! So your idea is no better than mine."

"Okay, girls, hold up. I think you both have hit the same jackpot and you don't even know it," Mr. Tolaez reinserted himself to cool the conversation. "I think this is a crucial point to understand: no human being was around at the time of creation. So how do we really know what happened? Science is about observing, measuring, and running experiments to prove something or to verify that something is repeatable. But we can't repeat the origin of the cosmos, can we? So many scientists actually accept evolution *by faith*. We Christians have the Bible. And we believe God's Word to be truth—divinely inspired and inerrant. So we accept God's Word, by the power of the Holy Spirit, *by faith*. Therefore, both the theory of evolution and creationism are matters of faith."

"No, they're not," Enola insisted.

"Yes, they are," interjected Tolaez. "But you are illustrating one main difference in the battle of worldviews: one side admits its argument is based on faith, and the other doesn't. Evolutionists say their argument is based on scientific fact, even when it's not. At least Christians admit they believe that the world was created by God by faith. Remember the shark teeth example? It's all a matter of interpretation and a worldview battle for sure." He paused. "So what I say to people who believe in evolution is, 'Hey, you have a faith and I have a faith, so let's talk about our faiths.'"

"Well, I don't believe creationism is based on science, so I can't trust it," Enola asserted. "Science just makes sense and is so provable. Think of where we would be without science, Mr. Tolaez."

"I hear you, Enola," Tolaez said. "I love science. It's led to so many cures, medicines, and improvements in our lives, to be sure. I thank God for science!" Then he added, "But have you ever noticed that what is accepted as science changes from time to time too?" Enola looked perplexed. "When I was growing up," Mr. Tolaez explained, "eggs were good for you. Then when I was in college, people said eggs were not so healthy for you. Now, scientists and nutrition experts are back to saying eggs are good for you, in moderation—you know, not eating too much or too little. I could say the same about coffee, running, certain immunizations and shots, and many other things. Scientists have changed their views on things over time and after new testing."

"That's the beauty of God's Word, Enola," Rennis interrupted. "It never changes. It's the same yesterday, today, and forever."

"Amen to that," said Tolaez. "And here at St. Peter's Lutheran School, we teach truth. We teach God's Word. The Bible says that God created the world in a very particular and orderly fashion. Human beings were created in God's image—unique and apart from the rest of His creations.

We didn't go from being an amoeba, to a fish, to a frog, and then to a human being by accident over billions of years with some mutations and squirrel hair mixed in to boot." Some kids laughed. "We were made in God's image. That's why we live with purpose, because God made each of you on purpose, not by chance or mistake. He sent His Son, Jesus, to die for each of you, not some cheetah or beetle or mosquito. You were made in His image. And you are His son or daughter."

Rennis Demeeder smiled and nodded as Mr. Tolaez concluded his lesson, while Enola Rettam frowned and continued to shake her head.

World Geography

The first chapter of their new textbook contained a lot of information on Pangaea—the hypothetical supercontinent that included all current landmasses and is believed to have been in existence before the continents split apart millions and millions of years ago. Rennis waited to hear how her teacher, Mr. Thomas Nagas, might address the "millions and millions of years ago" comment—which Mr. Tolaez had previously warned and taught was code language for evolution. "Do you think the great flood might have been the cause of this landmass breaking apart?" she asked Mr. Nagas, hoping he would provide some biblical context on the whole concept of Pangaea.

"Well, no one knows for sure why Pangaea split apart, Rennis," he responded. "But most geologists and scientists believe something caused it millions and millions of years ago. And it makes sense if you understand the continental drift theory—why our continents ended up in the locations they are today."

Rennis looked over at Enola, who was nodding and had a big grin on her face.

Health

Mrs. Alicia Rednow was showing the eighth-grade girls slides of the female body. "God created male and female," she asserted. "Not only did He make them unique, but He also made them to complement one another."

"Is it true, Mrs. Rednow," asked one student, "that God created women to be helpers of men?"

"Well, yes," she answered, knowing where the student really wanted to go. "In Genesis, God says that He created Eve to be a helper to Adam."

"That's not fair!" blurted out one young lady.

"Well, girls, hold on now. You and I both know that boys and men need a lot of help, isn't that right? It just shows how smart God was to know this from the very beginning." The girls laughed at Rednow's winsome humor. "But I like to think that since God made Eve from Adam's rib, He wants them—both husband and wife—to walk throughout life side by side with each other, together in harmony. After all, our God says that husband and wife are to become one flesh." The girls leaned in a bit more. Mrs. Rednow knew her presentation was beginning to drift off course, albeit into intriguing content for these young girls. "But we'll talk about that part later in the course!"

Science

The images from the *National Geographic* video on the various animal kingdoms around the world were spectacular. Rennis noticed, however, that her science teacher, Mr. Steven Llud, never said anything when the videos mentioned how animals evolved or learned survival instincts over millions and millions of years of evolution. Was that part true? The video sure seemed to make logical sense on that matter. Last week, Mr. Llud showed a clip from the movie *Jurassic World* as a hook for his new lesson. He did not say anything then either, however, when the movie clip referenced evolution and the survival of the fittest. Rennis had to admit she loved the *Jurassic World* movies and that the scenes in the *National Geographic* video were incredible. Enola seemed to love the videos too.

Math

Unpacking another intriguing faith connection or devotion in her math class, Mrs. Brittany Atad had already read from Genesis and other New Testament passages on how God created the heavens and earth and how all of creation is His handiwork. On her interactive whiteboard, she illustrated that the calculations of evolution being true were 1 to the power of 1 followed by zeros too numerous to count. "Those are the odds that evolution could be true. Does anyone want to take those odds?" she asked the class. Everyone but Enola shook their heads no. Finishing with a movie clip from the classic movie *Dumb and Dumber*, Mrs. Atad closed her message with the scene in which actor Jim Carrey, hoping to score a date with a pretty young lady, responds after she tells him that his chances of dating her are one in a million: "So you're saying there's a chance!" he says excitedly. Everyone except Enola laughed. Message received.

English

"I know you're both unhappy with my decision, but Rennis—you will be researching and presenting a persuasive speech in favor of evolution. Enola—you will be making the case for creationism," said Mrs. Carrie Rulb. "I know how strongly you each feel about this topic, but that's why I'm making you research the other side. This will broaden your horizons and perspective on this issue. And both sides of this issue are very viable positions to have, if I may say so." Mrs. Rulb thought her comments were helpful and inspiring to her two students of deep convictions. Rennis and Enola both frowned.

Art

"Remember, now," Mrs. Eve Nigiro said on the last day of the unit, "you made these projects out of clay. They are your creations. I can't wait for your parents to see them at our art fair next week." She paused and then picked up her Bible. "You know, many of you told me how proud or attached you are to your project. Well, your project is not even a living thing. Just think about how God thinks of you—His creation. Let me read a verse to you from Isaiah 64:8: 'But now, O Lord, You are our Father; we are the clay, and You are our potter; we are all the work of Your hand.'" Mrs. Nigiro looked up and saw all of her students' eyes on her. "God created each of you on purpose," she affirmed. "You're His masterpiece."

Reflection and Discussion

Did you notice the play on some of the names in this story? *Enola Rettam* spelled backward is *Matter Alone*, which is what most evolutionists believe is the extent of our existence. *Rennis Demeeder* spelled backward is *Redeemed Sinner*—what Christians know through the power of the Holy Spirit and the truth that is found only in God's Word. The name of the theology instructor, Mr. *Tolaez*, is *Zealot* spelled backward, as in being zealous for the truth. Geography teacher Mr. *Nagas* is *Sagan* spelled backward, as in Carl Sagan, the famed scientist and well-known proponent of evolution. The name of the health teacher, Mrs. *Rednow*, spelled backward is *Wonder*, which reminds each of us how we are fearfully and wonderfully made by God. The name of the science teacher, Mr. *Llud*, is *Dull* spelled backward, because his senses were dulled to the specific content he was allowing into his class. The name of the math teacher, Mrs. *Atad*, is *Data* spelled backward, as in the data that mathematicians, even non-Christian ones, use to conclude that evolution is almost mathematically impossible and that one kind cannot possibly change to another kind. The English teacher's name, Mrs. *Rulb*, spelled backward is *Blur*, as in blurring the lines of legitimacy for both evolution and creationism. The art teacher's name, Mrs. *Nigiro*, spelled backward is *Origin*, which is a good reminder that we originated not randomly through mutations over eons of time but were created on purpose by God. What are some cultural or societal issues or mores that the secular world has completely backward compared to what God teaches us in the Scriptures?

1. In regard to evolution and creationism, read some of the various Bible passages (Genesis 1; Hebrews 11:3; Colossians 1:16; John 1:1–3; Psalm 89:11; Psalm 19:1; Romans 1:18–23; 2 Timothy 4:3–4; Psalm 14:1; 1 Peter 3:15) in regard to God's creation of the world. What were some inadvertent mixed messages given by the teachers of St. Peter's Lutheran School? What might be the ramifications of these mixed messages?
2. What mixed messages might you as a teacher, administrator, or school be inadvertently sending to your students or constituents in regard to faith and mission?
3. What can you do to identify or recognize mixed messages when they occur? What can you do to align the mission properly so that there are no mixed messages?

A TEACHER AND A STANDARDIZED DREAM

BY BERNARD BULL

Allen wanted to be a teacher ever since he was in Mr. Bagley's class in fifth grade. Bagley taught at the same school his entire career. On the weekends, he played organ for the church across the street. During the week, he poured all of his time and energy into loving and teaching the students in his class. Each morning, Mr. Bagley greeted every student at the door by name, offering some kind of genuine affirmation to each person. Bagley knew each student and noticed even the slightest change. If a student got a new haircut, Bagley noticed it and managed to say something that made the student feel a little less self-conscious about it. If a student had a sick parent, he went out of his way to share an extra encouraging word.

Mr. Bagley rarely lectured the students, opting instead for hands-on experiments and experiences followed by his gentle guidance and short talks and group discussion. He valued curiosity and showed it by being deeply curious himself about pretty much anything and everything. For Allen, Mr. Bagley represented the best of being a teacher, and he couldn't wait to grow up and become the next Mr. Bagley. He worked hard in school, eventually went off to get a teaching degree at the state university, and then he excitedly applied to jobs in the area. He was ecstatic when he was called in for an interview at the very school where he once sat in the class with Mr. Bagley. Even better, he got the job and found himself assigned to the exact classroom in which he used to sit as a fifth grader.

Allen could not wait to begin this new job. It was not long before the first day of mandatory faculty in-service prior to the start of the school year. When he arrived, he was troubled by what he heard and saw. There was very little talk about making a difference in the lives of young people and the sorts of ideas that inspired him to teach in the first place. Instead, most of what he heard was the long list of rules and policies, the need to prepare students carefully for the standardized tests, and the importance of not deviating from the provided curriculum. As one person explained, "We only have so many hours in the day and days in the week, and our reputation depends on how well we prepare students for high school. So, make that your top priority, your second priority, and your third priority. Of course, we are a Christian school, and that is at the center of everything that we do; however, when it comes to academics, we measure our results by how students perform on the standardized tests, so keep that in mind."

This wasn't completely new to Allen. He certainly learned about the importance of standardized tests in his education program. He had helped out in many schools during his college years, but his student teaching was actually in a charter school that made curiosity and the love of learning their core and driving values. They used standardized tests as they were required, but the tests were certainly not the focal point. Yet Allen found himself in a Christian school where standardized tests and standards seemed to reign supreme. When he expressed his disappointment, one veteran teacher simply replied, "Welcome to the new normal in education."

It was a deflating start to Allen's career, but it didn't deter him. He studied the standards and curriculum and dutifully prepared for the first weeks of class. He stayed up late each night preparing each lesson, taking care to align everything that he was doing with the standards. However, he also grappled with how he could infuse a fair share of curiosity and the love of learning as well. He decided that he was going to try to create the best of both worlds. He would teach to the standards and prepare students for the tests, but he was also going to devote ample class time to exploration and experimentation. He did just that.

The first day of school, Allen welcomed the students at the door, introducing himself and working hard to memorize each student's name. Allen remembered the power of knowing and sharing names from Mr. Bagley years ago, so he had spent years refining his skill at remembering names. In fact, by the end of the first class period, he knew every student by name. By the end of the first week, he knew at least three to five facts about each student. Each day, he tried to learn more, and he worked hard at showing the students how much he cared about them and how committed he was to their learning.

He started every day with some sort of riddle or puzzle, even if just for a few minutes. Each one was carefully designed to spark some curiosity, capture their interest, and get the students thinking about the key idea for the day and why it was important for them to learn. After that activity, he introduced students to the topic for the day in a more formal way. He shared the goals and standards that would shape their work together. Just as expected by the school and district, he followed the curriculum carefully. He used the practice exams. He did the formal test preparation. He did all of it. Yet he found a way to do all of that in about half of each class, spending the other half doing what he considered more interesting and meaningful learning activities.

It wasn't what Allen dreamed of doing. He still lamented what sometimes felt like wasted class time focused upon preparing for a test. He wondered about the value of some of the topics required in the curriculum. Yet he carved out enough space to do the things that really mattered to him and that he believed to be valuable for his students.

He did this for the first quarter and, while still refining some of his skills as a teacher, ran a pretty good class. Students were engaged. They were showing good progress. There were minimal discipline issues.

Things were going pretty well. Allen cared about the students, and they knew it. He had more than a few opportunities to be there for students struggling with any number of life challenges. He also loved seeing his students' spark of interest and those "Aha!" moments when they learned something new.

This continued through the first year and every year after, until Allen found himself one of the more veteran teachers, with fifteen years of experience. Now a thirty-seven-year-old teacher, Allen hadn't lost his love of students and learning. Things were not perfect, and there were days when it was hard not to be discouraged or angry about some of the decisions made by leadership, but he was largely able to close the door and do his own thing. In fact, Allen did this for the rest of his career. He spent decades in the same school and classroom, adjusting to ongoing changes, rules, and standards. Yet he was able to navigate them because he kept two things front and center: he loved kids and he loved learning. For Allen, that was really all that mattered.

Reflection and Discussion

Most Christian and independent schools do not face as many of the mandates or pressures related to standardized tests. However, the challenge remains of aligning work with standards and meeting outside expectations.

1. To what extent do you see outside standards and expectations as putting pressures on how and what you teach?
2. Read Matthew 22:15–22. How does this passage influence your understanding of this topic?
3. How do you balance meeting external standards and expectations with your school's distinct mission and your desire to create a rich and engaging learning experience for students?
4. Allen found a way to work within the constraints of his school. To what extent do you find yourself having constraints, and how do you creatively design your classroom to respect those while also pursuing more creative or innovative practices?

THE HEART OF THE MATTER

Responding to an Unexpected Death within the School Community

BY MICHAEL UDEN

The rhythm of each day appealed most to Jesse Walker. That is not to say that each day was patterned or monotonous. For a high school biology teacher and cross-country coach, Mr. Jesse Walker's ten years of ministry at Community of Christ Lutheran High School had brought him much joy due to the elements on which he could count: teaching content he loved, being active and involved in numerous aspects of his school, and building and maintaining relationships with the students and families he served. Yet just like the uneven terrain of a cross-country course, each year of his teaching had been different, with its unique ruts and unexpected inclines. Still, God had blessed him with a supportive school community and many opportunities to see the Holy Spirit at work within his ministry, so Jesse Walker kept running the race before him.

He had run into colleagues in the hallway during his trek for morning coffee, and now he was late for his third-hour advanced biology class. Jesse winced as he worked to beat the tardy bell to his own class, since he routinely emphasized the importance of being fully present to both his students and athletes. Walker stressed to his protégés that soft skills, such as punctuality, coupled with life skills, including devoting one's full effort and attention to the task at hand, were a winning combination in the marathon of life. His students apparently remembered the lesson, as evidenced by their playful snickers upon Mr. Walker's entrance to the classroom. Quickly scanning the room to take attendance, he noticed only one student—Lucas Williamson—was absent. The topic du jour was muscle memory, and Mr. Walker's passion as an athlete melded well with his scholarly interest in the subject. After a brief lecture to provide an overview of the material and a compelling clip from a related documentary, Jesse had arranged his class of juniors and seniors into groups for a lab activity. The room emanated its frequent and harmonious hum of engaged and inquisitive students, and Mr. Walker was particularly pleased that he had recovered from a late start that period.

As the class bell rang again, Mr. Walker's mind quickly contemplated the setup he needed to complete during his upcoming prep hour before his fifth-hour freshman biology class. His characteristic focus was interrupted by a group of his students who had stayed past the bell.

"Mr. Walker," Tanner Johnston, one of his cross-country runners, began, "can we talk to you for a minute?"

One lesson Jesse Walker had learned in his ten years of teaching was to prioritize people. Ministry often happens in ways and at times one would not expect, and the tone of Tanner's voice, coupled with the expressions of his companions, led Jesse to believe this was more than a question regarding the homework assignment.

"Of course, guys," Jesse welcomed. "What's up?"

"Lucas was not in class today." Tanner paused.

"Is he okay?" Mr. Walker inquired.

"Well, I don't know. He hasn't been texting much this morning," Lucas's friend Tanner continued. "I do know something happened last night. In his family. His parents wanted him to stay home today."

"Do you gentlemen know what happened with the Williamsons?" Jesse inquired gently.

"Yeah," Stephen Holbert, another of Lucas's friends and a four-year cross-country runner, continued. "His brother Erik died last night. From an overdose. Heroin." Stephen spoke haltingly and in nearly a whisper.

Jesse braced himself on the table next to which he was standing. Now replaying in his mind a conversation he had overhead in the teacher's lounge not even an hour before, he recalled overhearing "Erik Williamson" in hushed tones. His heart sank.

Erik had been a student at Community of Christ Lutheran High School when Jesse had first accepted the call. He had not been on the cross-country team, but he was a student in Mr. Walker's classroom. Jesse could recollect his earnest nature and easy laugh. He was more outgoing than his far younger brother, Lucas, who was characteristically quiet and studious, even at cross-county practice. Jesse ached at the shock and pain he knew Lucas was processing.

While he had not kept up with what Erik Williamson had been doing since high school, he did recall seeing him at some of Lucas's meets during his freshman year. It struck Jesse how easy it was to lose track of students once they graduated from Community of Christ. What had become of Erik Williamson?

"I did not know Erik struggled with addiction," Mr. Walker responded. "My heart goes out to Lucas and his family."

"Some people say it was on purpose, Mr. Walker," Tanner declared. "Like, Erik was mad and frustrated with his life and with himself, so he wanted to die. Not an accidental overdose, but on purpose," Tanner's voice finished, but his eyes continued to communicate the hurt, concern, and uncertainty he felt.

"Suicide is unforgivable. Right, Mr. Walker?" Stephen's apparent frustration was matched only by the desperation in his voice.

"Guys, first, we do not know the details of the situation. We also do not know what was going on in Erik's mind and heart at the time of his death. Only God knows that. What we do know is that Lucas and his family are hurting, and we can and should reach out to them." Jesse had shared similar pronouncements far more often in a ten-year career than he could have ever imagined, yet the words still often sounded, even to him, as if he were reading them from a cue card.

The friends of Lucas Williamson who had assembled in Jesse Walker's classroom that day seemed to find purpose in his gentle admonition nonetheless. As Mr. Walker wrote out passes for them to enter their next class, they were coordinating plans to stop by the Williamsons' home after school and check in on Lucas. Jesse found himself reliving his first direct brush with suicide. A close college friend, Clarissa Maines, with whom Jesse had led youth ministry lock-ins and laughed his way through choir tours, overdosed on pills the summer before their senior year. He remembered getting a call from her mother, inviting him to the memorial service, "because he had been such a close friend." He also remembered how hard it had been to enter the doors of that church. Part of it was the surreal nature of the situation—the juxtaposition of a beautiful August afternoon and the deep and heavy emotion that enveloped him as he entered the church building. Part of it was the palpable anger he felt toward Clarissa. He had thought they were friends. Good friends. Yet for all they had shared with each other, why had she never shared all that she had been carrying and considering?

After the memorial service, Jesse had felt obligated to offer condolences to Clarissa's parents, although he wanted nothing more than to bolt from the church. As he hugged Clarissa's mother, she reached into the purse behind her and gave Jesse a note written to him by Clarissa before her death. Jesse was stunned, and it took him nearly a week to muster up the courage—or forgiveness—to open it. It was strange to see her handwriting and read words of both apology and thanks. Tears flowed as he mourned the loss of his friend for the first time and pictured her feeling so very alone when she wrote his note. In that moment, Jesse realized firsthand how hard Satan works to erode the hearts and minds of those not yet fully within his grasp.

While Jesse still could not understand what would bring a person to that place of desperation, he recognized the love and support needed for those left behind. He relived the guilt he felt months later, when he was laughing with high school students during a senior lock-in event and remembered that Clarissa was never again going to have that experience. He also recalled how Clarissa's pastor had directly spoken God's truth in love on the day of her funeral. The passage he read from Isaiah 41:10 in the service was still fresh in his mind. "Fear not, for I am with you; be not dismayed, for I am your God; I will strengthen you, I will help you, I will uphold you with My righteous hand." In the service that day, he spoke the word *suicide* from the pulpit, to Jesse's surprise and to the apparent discomfort of those sitting near him. Yet the pastor also reminded the congregation that Clarissa's spiritual state at the time of her death was known only by God. He spoke words of hope and grace to survivors who felt hopeless and heavy laden by ideas of Law and unforgivable sin. He reminded those gathered about the power and poignancy of the Body of Christ gathered in that sanctuary, and how their presence and support would be Christ's hands and feet in the days, weeks, and years ahead—not only to Clarissa's family but also to all with whom they would intersect. That commission had stuck with him and was playing in his mind as he reentered the faculty lounge for his lunch break.

A group of veteran teachers, all of whom had worked with Erik Williamson when he was a student at Community of Christ, were gathered at one table, comparing what they had heard about his untimely death. The tone of their reactions appeared as discordant as the assortment of coffee mugs he passed on his way to join the conversation.

"Drugs. What is it with people and drugs? How do people get so mixed up with these things?"

"I cannot believe it was a suicide. Erik had too much to live for; he was too blessed to give that all up."

"Erik and Lucas are two very different people. I remember Erik from his first day in my class, and he always had a lost look in his eyes. I wish I could say this surprises me at all."

Jesse stopped dead in his tracks before speaking his thoughts aloud. "A family in our community is facing an unimaginable tragedy. These parents are outliving one of their children. A younger brother is now an only child. We can speculate about the reasons and the details, or we can reach out and love them as Christ's hands and feet. Read the marquee outside: it says, 'Community of Christ Lutheran High School.' That is our mission, that is our calling, and we had better be about His business." Mr. Walker exited the lounge and returned to his classroom. He felt absolutely out of rhythm and emotionally spent.

The day continued for Jesse Walker, chronologically at least. He completed the rest of his assigned teaching and facilitated the after-school sports conditioning program, but his mind was with Lucas Williamson and, perhaps, with Clarissa Maines.

Returning back to his classroom before leaving for the day, Jesse was only somewhat surprised to encounter his morning crew—Lucas's cluster of friends—once again.

"Mr. Walker," Tanner began, "we are going to Lucas's house to hang out tonight. Do you want to come?"

"I . . ." Jesse Walker felt fully present for the first time since lunch.

"We think you should be there," Stephen volunteered. "You got me thinking a lot this morning, Mr. Walker, about how only God knows what was in Erik's heart and mind and that we should be caring for those who are hurting as the Body of Christ. We want Lucas to know that we are in his corner and that we are going to walk with him through this and find the new normal, whatever that might look like."

Mr. Walker smiled, recognizing how the Holy Spirit had used not only his words from earlier in the day but also the things he had not said but that Stephen had clearly heard and learned through others. Stephen's reminder—that the Holy Spirit works in, through, and in spite of us—was the familiar rhythm that Jesse so desperately needed to regain on a day when he had lost his footing and felt off-balance.

"I think it is a great idea for us to go to the Williamsons, to check in," Mr. Walker accepted Stephen's invitation.

"But I don't know what I am supposed to say," confessed Michael Budd, who had been a part of Lucas's impromptu support team but had been apart from the others in his countenance. "I have never had someone close to me die, and I don't want to say something wrong."

"You don't need to feel like you have to say anything, Michael," Mr. Walker reassured him. "Your presence will mean a lot to Lucas, whether you speak or not. It's also okay to talk about school today or the prom next month or getting pizza later. You're each a part of a new chapter in Lucas's life that feels completely foreign to him right now. The only danger would be in not being there."

"Thanks," Michael exhaled.

As they walked to the parking lot, Jesse Walker shared a recollection from Clarissa Maines's funeral service. It was of her younger brother, who at the time was probably about the same age as Lucas's friends, who sat alone in the pew and stood alone in the receiving line after the memorial service.

"Didn't his friends show up?" Tanner wondered aloud.

"No, they were there," Jesse replied. "Much of Clarissa's hometown was there, and certainly her church family. Yet they did not know what to say, or they were afraid that they might say something wrong," he continued, looking briefly at Michael, "so they said nothing and did not even approach their friend, Clarissa's brother."

"That is cold-hearted," Stephen assessed.

"I don't know what was in their hearts," Mr. Walker acknowledged, "but I suspect it was fear or uneasiness more than apathy. The point is that we have the chance to be Christ's hands and feet to the Williamson family, today and in the days and weeks ahead. We may not feel we know what to do or what to say, but doing nothing and saying nothing will communicate a far stronger message. We are called simply to love, not to judge Erik's heart or motive. Simply to love."

"You are an awesome teacher, Mr. Walker," Michael replied. "And not just about biology. Thanks for going with us."

"Thanks for the invitation, guys. It is a real blessing to be part of Community of Christ Lutheran High School. Death is a lot different for those who know Christ and have the promise of life everlasting."

"We know," Tanner affirmed.

The three cars of their convoy arrived at the Williamson home at the same time, and the occupants exited the vehicles and seemingly assembled before making their way to the front door. Stepping on the porch, Jesse looked back and was surprised to see a carful of his break room colleagues pulling up to the curb, emerging with casseroles in hand. Their eyes met his, and the exchange communicated simultaneous regret, forgiveness, and resolve.

The first wave from Community of Christ Lutheran High School rang the doorbell. Lucas Williamson answered, and his initial expression metamorphosed upon seeing his closest friends and his coach,

Mr. Walker. “We are so sorry for your loss, Lucas. We came to tell you how much we care and to be with you in person for a little while,” Jesse Walker began. The Body of Christ entered the home, where life was affirmed and renewed.

Reflection and Discussion

Scripture provides many examples of God's healing and care during times of trauma and tragedy. Read and reflect on the following Scripture passages as part of this chapter discussion: Isaiah 41:10; Psalm 147:3; Psalm 23:4; Galatians 6:2; Revelation 21:4.

1. While drug addiction, drug overdose, and suicide are familiar components of our culture, many Christians are uncomfortable discussing these topics directly. To what do you attribute the discomfort, and should Christians' collective level of candor change?
2. Recount a time when you experienced an unforeseen tragedy. How did you want those closest to you to respond?
3. Mr. Walker spoke specifically to his students and colleagues about how the school community should respond to such a tragedy. What is the danger in a Christian school of not taking such a direct stance?
4. Ephesians 4:15 directs Christians to "[speak] the truth in love." Where was that evident—or lacking—in this case study?

CHAPTER 6

LIDS

Why Pastors Can't Be Women

BY JIM PINGEL

MONDAY

Out of all of his duties and responsibilities as the associate pastor of Bethlehem Lutheran Church and School, teaching theology class to seventh and eighth graders in the Christian day school remained one of Pastor Joel Peck's favorite. Middle school students were curious, blunt, and impressionable. Moreover, they asked good questions, and Pastor Peck wondered if these questions were on the hearts and minds of his entire congregation too.

Pastor Peck's love for his students and his joy for teaching them were two reasons why many students at Bethlehem regarded him as their favorite teacher. "Pastor P is like me," many students told their parents. Indeed, Pastor Peck specialized in engagement and connecting students to God's Word. He enjoyed sports, outdoor recreational activities, movies, and a good joke. He took time to get to know each student on a personal level, and he listened to their concerns, joys, sorrows, and frustrations earnestly and patiently. Most important, as a father of three young children, he knew what kids needed most—Jesus. Teaching students God's Word in all its truth and purity energized him, and he remained grateful that God saw fit to use him as an instrument of His mercy, grace, and love.

Since Pastor Peck knew that most students enjoyed him as a teacher, he tried to guard against the ego creep that seemed to confound so many other pastors. Whether he was beloved or not, he would remain steadfast in teaching God's Word. "I am called to serve God and not man," he reminded himself daily. Yet as a sinful human being, he had to admit that he liked being liked. The affirmation he received from his students and their parents made him feel good and lifted his self-esteem. What a blessing to serve at Bethlehem!

One day early in September, little Jimmy Sipe, a seventh grader, stayed after class instead of heading home. "What can I do for you, Jimmy?" Pastor Peck asked.

"Well, Pastor," Jimmy spoke rather softly. "You know how much I like you." Indeed, Pastor Peck received almost weekly emails from Jimmy's parents telling him how much he meant to Jimmy and their family. Pastor P was Jimmy's favorite teacher ever, hands down.

"I like you too, Jimmy," he quickly rejoined. "So what's on your mind?"

"Well, you know how you were talking about submission today when we were reading Ephesians 5 in class, and how the man is supposed to be the head of the household, and then all that stuff you said about pastors can only be guys and stuff."

"Yes," Pastor Peck interrupted, slowly trying to follow the middle schooler's run-on sentences. He could see Jimmy fidgeting and growing more uncomfortable by the second.

"Well, a few of the new eighth-grade girls in the back of the room were kind of getting sassy about it. They don't think it's right that girls can't be pastors or that girls have to let men be the boss of them. One even said her mom would not agree with anything you were saying at all." Jimmy rattled off the words quickly as he lifted his burden on to the pastor.

"Oh," said Pastor Peck. He paused to ponder. "Was it Ashley and Olivia who were saying those things?"

"Yeah," said Jimmy. "And I don't want them to get in trouble. Please, Pastor, don't say anything to them. I just thought . . ." Now Jimmy paused. "I just thought you might want to know. Maybe you can, like, tell a story or talk about why we believe what we believe." In truth, Jimmy did not quite understand why women could not be pastors. They could be everything else, it seemed—CEOs, doctors, teachers, attorneys, governors, senators, managers, business owners, school principals, rock stars, movie stars, even pastors in other churches or on television. His own mother was a prominent financial analyst at First Community Bank in town. And *Wonder Woman* was one of his favorite movies. Why couldn't women be pastors too?

"Well, Jimmy," Pastor Peck calmly responded. "Thank you so much for letting me know. I know Ashley and Olivia just transferred here this fall from the local public school. They don't understand how we do things around here or why we believe what we believe. We'll just have to be patient with them and pray for them, okay?"

"But don't you think we or you need to do something?" Jimmy insisted. "They were saying, 'Whatever!' when you were talking and being kind of rude to you. I don't think they will like you or listen to you if you don't tell them why women can't be pastors. Just tell them why!" Jimmy was troubled that his favorite teacher did not seem to understand. The lack of respect and snide remarks made about Pastor Peck truly bothered him.

"I'll tell you what," Pastor Peck replied. "Let me pray and think about the best way to handle this." Touched by Jimmy's concern, Pastor Peck made a mental note to talk about women's roles in the Church and in the home later in the week.

"Okay, thanks for listening, Pastor. It just bothered me, I guess."

"Hey, Jimmy," Pastor Peck said, "thanks for caring. You have a good Monday now. See you tomorrow in class."

Tuesday

"Do you have a minute?" Principal Jill Holtmeier asked as she stepped into Pastor Peck's classroom. Pastor Peck and Principal Holtmeier loved working together. Jill Holtmeier's respect for the pastoral office, as well as her confidence and steady leadership, truly impressed Peck. Unlike some other Lutheran school principals he knew, Jill Holtmeier never seemed to feel threatened or worried about being undercut in her leadership role by having a pastor on staff. Conversely, Principal Holtmeier appreciated the pastor's winsome ability to welcome non-Lutheran students with warm and open arms. He taught all students the truth, to be sure, but he did it without making students of other denominations or faith outlooks feel inferior or less important. Moreover, Pastor Peck did not want to be the titular or even de facto leader of the school; he wanted only to be a teacher who could make an eternal impact on the faith lives of his students.

"Sure, what's up?" Pastor Peck responded.

"You probably haven't checked your email yet, but I forwarded you an email I got from a Ms. Karen Barrett, the mother of one of your students—Olivia?"

"Yes, I have Olivia in class. She's one of the new transfers to our school. What's it about?" Pastor Peck inquired, with a hunch that he already knew.

"Well, I'll let you read it, but apparently you were teaching about the relationships between men and women, why pastors can't be women, and, well, she didn't like it much. She's wondering if this is our official position as a school and threatening to transfer Olivia to another school if that's the case."

"She just transferred in, and after a few weeks, they'll take Olivia right out?" Pastor Peck asked with dismay.

"Apparently there is no 'they,'" Jill Holtmeier continued. "You'll see in the email. Karen is divorced because her ex-husband cheated on her. She goes through some of the details in her email."

"Well, what did you tell her?" Pastor Peck asked.

"I wrote her back saying that we practice Matthew 18 at Bethlehem Lutheran School, and that she needs to talk directly to you about this. I just came down here to let you know about it and offer my support." She added, "In my experience with these kinds of situations, I would be surprised if she called you. Do you mind taking the initiative to call her during your prep period today? You're always so good at dealing with these kinds of situations."

"Of course I will," Pastor Peck replied. "I guess I'll also need to make sure Olivia doesn't feel uncomfortable in class today too," he reflected. "Does Olivia know her mom sent an email complaining about what I taught in class?"

"She didn't say in the email."

"Okay, well thank you, Jill. It's never dull around here, is it?"

"No, it's not," Principal Holtmeier agreed. "Joel, remember: God put you here for a reason. And I, for one, am really glad He did. There's no one better equipped to handle these kinds of cultural issues than you. I'm glad you're here."

"Me too!" Pastor Peck responded with a dab of sarcasm. "At least, I think I am. I'll keep you in the loop about our conversation."

When Olivia walked into the classroom later that day, Pastor Peck made sure he greeted her warmly and kindly. "Hi," Olivia said without looking up. She immediately went to her desk, sat down, and made no eye contact for the rest of the class period. She did not even talk with Ashley. Her energy and moxie were gone.

Wednesday

After leaving two messages on Tuesday and not receiving a return call, Pastor Peck finally connected with Ms. Barrett on Wednesday evening. She probably did not recognize his cell phone number, Peck thought to himself, when she picked up his call. Pastor Peck had tried desperately to meet face-to-face with Olivia's mother because he felt these conferences offered a more intimate, personal way to connect. Ms. Barrett, however, had no desire to meet in person. She was a busy mom and business woman. This "unfortunate situation," she insisted, could be handled on the phone. Besides, she and Olivia had visited two other schools today, and they would be making a school decision by the end of the week. No wonder Olivia was absent today, thought Peck.

Ms. Barrett's belligerence surprised Pastor Peck. Ticking off one issue after another, Ms. Barrett argued that men keep women down and put up glass ceilings. Women make less money than men do even when they do the same jobs. Religious institutions kick women to the curb and suppress their voice and leadership capabilities. After conducting some research online, she asserted that the LCMS remained a "male-dominated industry and hierarchy" in an age of diversity. She wondered why women were not allowed to lead chapel at Bethlehem. She questioned why the girls' cross-country runners had to wear T-shirts over their sports bras but the guys could run shirtless. She purported that girls were more frequently penalized for dress code violations compared to boys. Did Pastor Peck think a woman could be a doctor, CEO, or the president of the United States? She assumed that many Christian schools might not support the LGBTQ movement, but she had no idea that the LCMS did not support a woman's right to choose or women's reproductive rights. When were they going to get out of the Stone Age? No wonder their church membership numbers were shrinking. As a business woman and financial advisor, she would not recommend schools such as Bethlehem as a place others should invest in, because their stock was "headed downward big time."

When Pastor Peck tried to shift the conversation to his class and Olivia, Ms. Barrett pounced. Did he really believe that women were supposed to submit to men? Should she stay home and bake cookies too? What about abusive, cheating men such as her ex? What did the good pastor have to say about men like that? And females could not be pastors? Weren't we in the twenty-first century? She had listened to some male pastors who were boring and had no leadership or management skills. Why not let a woman lead if she had the gifts?

Every time Pastor Peck tried to respond to one of her questions or barbs, Ms. Barrett cut him off or injected yet another aggressive rant. Pastor Peck wanted to explain what he was teaching Olivia and the other students and why. He wanted to share with her God's design and created order, how both men and women were to be submissive to God (submissiveness was a good thing, not a bad thing as the culture now taught), and how men were to give themselves up for their wives as Christ had done for the Church (Ephesians 5). Furthermore, Pastor Peck sensed that Ms. Barrett had been truly wronged and hurt by her ex-husband. Even in the midst of her verbal barrage, he felt compassion for her. When he offered Christian council and prayers for her, she responded courteously but firmly: "Oh, I appreciate your concern, but I can handle myself, thank you. I certainly don't need another man to help me. This isn't about me anyway, but about my daughter getting indoctrinated by antiquated values and an old-time religion. Lutherans put lids on ladies," she insisted.

Finally, at the end of the conversation, Pastor Peck managed to sneak out the words, "Please know, Ms. Barrett, that we care deeply for Olivia. We only want the best for her, and we think the best thing for her is a growing relationship with Jesus Christ and the eternal comfort found only in God's Word. We teach the truth here at Bethlehem, and I hope Olivia remains here to hear it."

The call ended abruptly, and Pastor Peck felt dejected. Craving the comfort of his God, he said a prayer for Karen, Olivia, and himself. Then entering the family room, he asked his wife, Alva Lea, "Honey, do you feel like our church keeps a lid on women?"

THURSDAY

"So you see, my fine ladies and gentlemen," Pastor Peck said to his religion class as he worked up a good lather, "being submissive is not a negative thing in the way it is too often portrayed in this world. Jesus Himself submitted to His heavenly Father in the Garden of Gethsemane and all the way to the cross—and thank God He did, otherwise He never would have accomplished His mission to cleanse us from our sins!" Pastor noticed Olivia gazing at him, while Jimmy, sitting behind Olivia, looked down at his notebook. "Yes, God's Word tells us that wives are to submit to their husbands, but husbands are to love their wives as Christ loved the Church," Pastor Peck continued. "Hey, folks, remember: Jesus died for the Church. Gentlemen, when you get married someday, you might want to remember the kind of sacrificial love God is calling you to show your special sweetheart!" The girls smiled, while some of the boys groaned. "That's right," Pastor continued, "a real Romeo is willing to lay down his life—to give his everything—for his Juliet. Ladies, don't worry; apparently God doesn't require you to give your life for your man." A few more smiles and laughs came from the girls and even more groans from the guys. After inserting a deliberate pause for his prime point, Pastor Peck summed it up: "God wants marriage to be a beautiful, loving relationship between one man and one woman, and each partner keeps his and her own special role." As Pastor Peck looked deliberately at Olivia, he was pleasantly surprised to see her looking directly at him. "Are there any other questions for our review today?"

"Pastor," Ashley piped up, "I still don't get why women can't be pastors. The verses you point out talk about women being silent or quiet in church. The women I know are definitely *not* silent in church!" Some of the students in class laughed out loud at Ashley's wit.

"It's not that they can't be pastors or are not capable of being a pastor," Pastor Peck said, somewhat surprisingly to Jimmy's ears. "It's that God, in His infinite wisdom, chose the pastoral role for men, just like He gave women the beautiful and distinctive role of carrying and giving birth to a child." Trying to lighten the mood, Pastor Peck continued, "Ashley, you and I can ask God that question someday when we get to heaven. Make no mistake, all men and women can teach and share the love of Christ and God's Word—and I pray that you will do that wherever you go."

After class ended, Olivia walked up to Pastor Peck and handed him her Bible. "I'm transferring to Central Middle School tomorrow, so I won't be needing this." Pastor Peck's heart raced. He had not connected with Olivia. She did not seem to like him, and that feeling bothered him more than he cared to admit. Why and how had he failed to connect with her?

"Olivia," he finally spoke up, "I'm sorry to hear that. I wish you would stay."

"Mom doesn't want me here, and I guess I don't want to be here either," she explained.

After an awkward pause, Pastor Peck said, "Why don't you keep your Bible? I want you to have it. It's God's precious Word for you."

"Pastor, I have nothing against you," Olivia shrugged. "My mom and I just don't believe in what this school teaches. It's kind of weird, and, well, it's a man's world out there, but that's changing. Girls have to support girls, you know."

"Olivia, before you go, can I pray for you?" Pastor Peck sounded almost desperate.

Olivia let a quick smile escape. "No, that's okay, Pastor. It's okay. Maybe I'll see you around town." She quickly left the room, her Bible lying on her teacher's desk.

FRIDAY

"I'm sorry, Pastor Peck," Jimmy said after class. "I know how much you care about all your students. If it makes you feel any better, I still think you're the best teacher in the world."

"Thanks, Jimmy," Pastor Peck said, eking out a partial smile. "Now I can sleep better tonight."

"Pastor Peck," interrupted Principal Holtmeier's voice, "do you have a few minutes to visit with Kim Theobald?"

"Sure," said Pastor Peck, "that's what I'm here for." As Jimmy waved goodbye and headed out the door, Pastor Peck pointed at him and said, "I'll see you in church on Sunday, young man." Jimmy nodded.

"Hi, Pastor Peck," said Kim. "I'm Ashley's mom."

"Oh, so very nice to meet you," Pastor Peck said as his heart rate picked up. "Ashley's a very bright young lady and a confident one too." The two shook hands.

"Oh!" Kim said, with a concerned look. "I hope not too confident."

"No, no, not at all. She asks good questions and is not afraid to ask them. I like that about her," Pastor Peck reassured. "Please sit down." Pastor Peck brought his chair out from his desk and sat in close proximity to Kim. As Principal Holtmeier walked out of the classroom, she gave Pastor Peck an encouraging smile.

"Well, speaking of questions, we are new to the whole religious school thing. But I have to tell you, Ashley really likes this school and she likes you." Pastor Peck took a deep breath. He wondered when the other shoe would drop. "But I have a few questions about some of the things you are teaching," Kim continued. "I believe Ashley can be and do anything she sets her mind to. So, well, we just want to understand better what you are teaching, because it's not the kind of thing you hear so much out there in the real world, you know? Do you have a few minutes to talk?"

Reflection and Discussion

Read the following Bible verses on the role of women in the Church and in the relationship God intends for husband and wife: 1 Corinthians 14:33–35; 1 Timothy 2:11–15; 3:8–13; Titus 1:5–6; 1 Peter 3:1–7; 1 Corinthians 11:1–16; Ephesians 5:22–33.

1. Why and how are some of these verses so countercultural today? Why is God's design for husband and wife so beautiful?
2. Which relationships in this story were most intriguing to you? Why?
3. How do you think Pastor Peck handled his predicament with Karen and Olivia Barrett? What would you have done differently?
4. Karen Barrett's character represents many of the current cultural issues or arguments made against mainline church denominations and their teachings on the vocations of women. Which of Barrett's barbs in particular are the most challenging to address in your opinion? Why? How do you or would you address them in your own context?
5. Pastor Peck could never get past the cultural and gender issues that Karen Barrett hurled at him on the phone in order to strike up a deeper conversation on faith. How can Christian teachers directly teach and address these cultural hot-button issues that cause so many to doubt or disdain the Christian faith and, at the same time, make sure these cultural issues do not overshadow the teaching of Law and Gospel?

A TALE OF BOREDOM DISRUPTED

From Sleeping to Dreaming

BY BERNARD BULL

It didn't matter whether she had ten hours or ten minutes of sleep, Brenda always dozed off in her first-hour class. She arrived on time each day, took her assigned seat in eighth-grade English, and proceeded to gradually, albeit sometimes abruptly, fall asleep. It was a class of thirty-five students, so the teacher usually didn't notice. In fact, Ms. Baxter only noticed twice in the entire first quarter, despite the fact that Brenda slept through at least ten to fifteen minutes of every class in the first seven weeks of the school year. Little did she know that she was soon to experience boredom disrupted.

She didn't mean to be rude or disrespectful. If you asked her why she fell asleep in class, she would just explain that she was always so tired during that first hour. She couldn't explain it. She didn't try to sleep. It just happened. Of course, she didn't try to avoid it either. She sat down, class started, and before she knew it her head was bobbing. Brenda didn't have any health issues. She slept well at night. She was not going through especially stressful challenges at home or school. It was just something about this first-hour class.

When it came to grades in the class, Brenda did okay. She stayed awake long enough to figure out what she needed to do for homework, and she borrowed notes from a friend to study for the tests. Fortunately, Ms. Baxter provided a study guide for every test, listing each item that needed to be studied. If you knew what was on the study guide, you would at least pass every test, if not get a B or higher.

As the first semester ended and the second semester started, Ms. Baxter assigned the students a short personal position paper. It was a simple, three- to five-page essay on a single statement: "Literature can save and destroy people's lives." She walked around the room with a hat, and each student had to pull a small piece of paper out of it. Each paper simply said "true" or "false." The paper that you picked determined the position that you had to take on the paper.

Brenda pulled out her piece of paper and opened it. It said "true." She glanced down at the instructions for the paper again and was a little confused. "Literature can save and destroy people's lives"? How could that possibly be true? These are just stories. How can a story save or destroy a life? She didn't sleep during that class, but she also didn't pay much attention for the rest of the session. Instead, she was mulling over this assignment, struggling to figure out how she would write a paper on something that was the complete opposite of her lived experience. Literature had little meaning to her, and she couldn't imagine how it could be influential enough to save or destroy a life.

With these thoughts on her mind, she did something for the first time in the school year. She stayed after class and had a one-on-one conversation with her teacher. She explained her dilemma. Ms. Baxter just smiled. "It sounds like you have your work cut out for you. Maybe you could start by trying to search for examples of influential pieces of literature from the past or present. See if you can find any novels or stories that had a large impact on people or communities."

That evening, Brenda experienced another first. It was the first time the entire year that she devoted any thought to literature class that was not focused on passing a test or doing just enough to complete an assignment and get a passing grade. She wasn't really thinking about the class at all. She was consumed and a little annoyed by this haunting question. Can literature really save or destroy a life?

Brenda took out her phone and decided to ask the electronic assistant a question: "Are there books that changed the world?" The electronic assistant misunderstood and opened a different app on her phone. Brenda decided to try an online search instead. This time she came up with a few interesting prospects. Browsing the first page of results, she noticed several references to a vaguely familiar book, *Uncle Tom's Cabin* by Harriet Beecher Stowe. As she did more research, she learned that many considered this book to be instrumental in raising awareness about the wrongs of slavery in America. One source even claimed that it was a key factor in leading up to the Civil War and the Emancipation Proclamation.

This fascinated Brenda. In a time when women's voices had less power in public spheres than today, this single woman writer wrote a book that contributed to the changing of a nation and undoubtedly saving many lives. It influenced people's views about human worth and value regardless of the color of a person's skin.

Brenda continued her search and found a large number of sources suggesting that the Bible is one of the most influential pieces of literature in history. Of course, she knew that it served as the foundation for the teachings of Christianity. As she continued to read, she became amazed at how the Bible influenced the larger world of art, literature, music, politics, and more. Until this time, Brenda never really thought about the Bible this way, nor did she think about the idea of a piece of writing actually having a significant impact upon the lives of people. "Is it really true that literature can be that powerful?" she wondered.

This was just the beginning for Brenda. Her initial research led to more searches and a growing list of books that changed the world. By bedtime, Brenda had a list of over thirty such books, with notes about the authors and how their books influenced people and saved lives, as well as a list of books that spread negative ideas that very likely led to the death of people. She even ordered a couple of the books through the local library and found a free copy of *Uncle Tom's Cabin* online. She started reading it that very night.

It was hard to read, since it was written in less familiar English, but she persisted. She wanted to know what was so special about it. It wasn't long before she read about people buying and selling people. It was a painful read; for the first time in her life, Brenda felt something when she read. She felt sadness and anger. She had felt moved by movies before, but never by a book. The more she read, the more she could imagine how a book such as this could influence people, how it could serve as a mirror for the conscience of people. She fell asleep reading the book, but this time it was not from boredom or disinterest. She didn't realize it, but she had been reading for hours, and she fell asleep in the early hours of the morning.

Needless to say, something changed for Brenda that day. It started with a simple question and assignment in class that, for one reason or another, conjured a deep interest and curiosity. Now Brenda was consumed with this question. There were times when she remained disinterested in what was happening in class on a daily basis, but each new story or book had a renewed interest for her. Each time there was a new reading, she had to wonder if this book, too, had saved a life, destroyed a life, or changed a person in some important way. In fact, while she was not quite ready to do the work, Brenda even found herself wondering about what it would take for her to write a book that would change the world.

Reflection and Discussion

1. Why was Brenda falling asleep in class?
2. Think about your own experiences as a student. Do you recall times when you fell asleep or found it very difficult to stay focused or alert? What was the cause?
3. While we can certainly expect that students take responsibility for paying attention in class, to what extent does this story illustrate the role of the teacher in helping to reduce the likelihood of boredom, sleeping, and disinterest?
4. As you consider students in your school, can you think of any who might be disinterested, bored, or falling asleep for similar reasons?
5. While it might seem too simple, the change for Brenda ultimately came from a simple question and associated challenging assignment. Consider what you are teaching over the next week, month, quarter, or year. What provocative questions or challenging assignments might aid students in deeper thinking and greater engagement in what you are teaching? As an exercise, consider writing a list of two to four such questions for each of the next few units that you plan to teach.
6. Questions are incredibly powerful tools for teaching and for learning, and the Scriptures demonstrate this tactic as well. Take some time to do a search for "questions asked in the Bible" or "questions Jesus asked." What can you learn about teaching and learning from these questions?

A TALE OF A GREAT TEACHER AND A GRADE AWAKENING

BY BERNARD BULL

Karen set high standards for her middle school science students, and she expected them to meet those standards. Little did she know that one year she would have a grade awakening. As a great teacher, Karen went out of her way to help students improve. Everybody knew this about her. Teachers and administrators respected her as a consummate professional. Students described her not only as one of the toughest teachers in the school but also as fair. Parents saw her this way too. They knew that she would push their son or daughter, and they also knew that Karen didn't tolerate parent complaints that were really just cloaked tactics to manipulate the teacher into lowering the academic bar or giving their child an unfair advantage.

Yet Karen wasn't the sort of teacher who graded on a curve. She was happiest when every student earned an A, although that never happened. She wanted every student to succeed. It was just that she was not about to create some sort of false sense of success by adjusting the bar for each student so that everyone could experience the joy of success. "The soul of the sluggard craves and gets nothing, while the soul of the diligent is richly supplied" (Proverbs 13:4). "Whoever works his land will have plenty of bread, but he who follows worthless pursuits lacks sense" (Proverbs 12:11). Both of these Bible verses were printed above the whiteboard in the front of her classroom, and they accurately conveyed her beliefs about teaching and learning.

Each day in class, Karen restated her expectations, driving students to work as hard as possible for the next major test, paper, or project. It was a relentless focus on improved performance and progress toward earning the highest possible grade on the test or assignment. There were no surprises. She told them exactly what they had to know and be able to do if they wanted to earn the highest grade. Then she worked with students individually and in groups to progress toward that goal.

For Karen, the best measure and motivator was the grade. A high grade meant high performance and a job well done. Therefore, she put a great deal of emphasis on students earning high grades in her class, and she took great care to explain clearly what went into earning the best grades. If you wanted an A in her class, then you had to earn A's consistently throughout, from the graded assignments in the first weeks all the way through the final exam. You had to follow the instructions carefully, turn things in on time, make positive contributions to the class, and much more. She carefully designed a grading system in her class to make sure that students did all of these things to earn a top grade. Again, she went out of her way to help students, but she was not about to lower or adjust her standards for anyone.

Because she believed so strongly in the grade as a measure of high performance, she spent lots of time finding the research to support this. She consistently shared this research about letter grades with the students. Students with high grade point averages in high school are more successful in college. They are more likely to get good grades in college and to persist through graduation. She found that grade point average correlated with happiness in life, positive habits and behaviors, even higher annual income after college. She shared these statistics with students and put posters of these facts on one wall of her classroom.

One year, two students left a lasting impression on Karen that challenged her to rethink her approach to grading and led to her personal grade awakening. Michelle and Michaela both arrived on the first day of class ready and excited to learn. Yet they had some major differences in their backgrounds.

Michaela came from a family that loved science. Her mother was a well-respected brain surgeon, and her dad was a professor of biology at the nearby state university. Since Michaela was born, her family vacations were a blend of recreation and research that took them around the world. She had swum with dolphins, gone scuba diving at the Great Barrier Reef, helped her dad collect samples to protect endangered species of birds in the Midwest (he was an ornithologist, and Michaela was probably the only student in the room who even knew what that word meant), and much more. Her parents had made sure that she was able to read and do basic math before even starting school; they introduced her to human anatomy and biology from the time she could speak. Michaela had an impressive collection of knowledge by the time she arrived in this first day of middle school science class. In many other schools, she would have skipped middle school science and jumped right to high school or AP biology, but despite Karen's lobbying for it, this small Lutheran school didn't offer such options.

Michelle grew up on the poor side of town. Her father passed away from a rare illness when she was eleven; her mom worked as a waitress in the evenings and on weekends and for a cleaning service during the weekdays. Michelle's mom made sure the two of them had everything they needed to get by, but there wasn't that much more. In fact, Michelle had been picking up babysitting jobs for some time, but her mom insisted that all of that money go into a savings account to help pay for college.

Michelle wanted to be a doctor one day. Initially inspired by seeing the healthcare workers care for her father, she wanted to be there for future families in such circumstances. In fact, for the past year, she volunteered at the local hospital through a new program for future healthcare workers. While Michelle and Michaela didn't know each other well, Michelle saw Michaela's mom fairly often at work, and she looked up to her. Michelle wasn't always a straight-A student, but she worked incredibly hard, especially since she set her mind on becoming a doctor. Every A took maximum effort and focus for Michelle. She didn't have the same sort of upbringing as Michaela, but both of them were excited for this science class.

When it came to the first day of Karen's science class, these two young women were excited and ready to get to work. Yet as the first couple of weeks developed, it was clear that they were having different experiences in the class. Most of the material was familiar to Michaela for the first several weeks. This was easy and undemanding, and she didn't need to do much to earn that A. This was far from the common experience in Karen's class, but it certainly elevated Michaela's confidence even more. She finished the first unit in the class with a perfect score—something that had never happened in Karen's class.

Michelle devoted hours studying those first weeks. She loved what she was learning and was fascinated with all of the key ideas. Yet the weekly quizzes and graded assignments were not easy for her, at least not at first. In fact, her grades in those first weeks were not nearly what she wanted or needed to accomplish her life goals. After the first unit test, Michelle had a C+. She started to doubt her ability to become a doctor one day, but she was not going to give up that easily. She set up a meeting with her teacher after school, explained the situation, and while holding back her tears, asked for advice.

Karen knew just what to do. She spent a couple of hours after school working with Michelle over the next week. It didn't take long for her to figure out the few misunderstandings and gaps in Michelle's prior knowledge that kept holding her back. Once they got these figured out, things started to work out much better for Michelle. She still spent three times as long studying for this class as Michaela did, but by the middle of the semester, Michaela and Michelle were competing for the top spot in class on each new unit test.

Of course, those first weeks continued to taint Michelle's grade. She knew that even if she got a perfect score on everything else in the class, her absolute best grade in the class would be a B+. However, she was committed to making that best outcome a reality, and she did just that. When it came time for the cumulative final examination, Michelle was the most prepared student in class. In fact, when the grading was finished, Michelle had achieved something that no other student had ever accomplished in Karen's course: she earned a perfect score on the final exam, with Michaela earning 93 percent, a very respectable second-highest grade in the class.

As Karen reflected on the year, she could say with confidence that Michelle was the hardest working and most focused student who had ever gone through this class. She also demonstrated the greatest level of mastery in the course. Yet she finished the class with a B+ because of those early grades. Michaela, on the other hand, was a very good student as well, but she just didn't put in the effort to achieve the level of mastery demonstrated by Michelle. Regardless, Michaela finished the class with a solid A+, while Michelle did not.

This bothered Karen, because she took the upmost pride in two key traits. She wanted to be a tough teacher with very high standards. She also wanted to be supremely fair. For her, this meant that the hardest working students with the highest level of mastery should be the ones with the highest grades, but this was clearly not the case when she looked at these two students. Something about this situation was not fair to Karen.

Neither Michelle nor Michaela seemed to mind the outcome. In fact, they both seemed quite happy with it. After all, they'd spent years in a school system where what they just experienced was the norm. They had both learned to work within the system, and it generally served both of them well.

While your average teacher might have mused about this for a little while and moved on, Karen could not let go of it. She saw this as a professional failure and began to examine carefully the performance of other students in the class as well. She consistently found that students with prior knowledge coming into the class did better than others, even when those others earned higher grades during the second half of the class and on the final exam. In other words, according to Karen, her class grading system favored the more advantaged students and penalized the students who needed the full time span of the course to perform at their best.

When the school year ended, Karen dedicated her summer to solving this problem. She read countless journal articles, reached out to assessment experts around the country, and built her own assessment expertise. At the end of her assessment, she decided that a key to solving this problem in her class was learning to make better use of ungraded and low-stakes feedback during the first half of the semester. As the class progressed, she would then add more graded and higher-stakes assessments. She also decided to experiment more with standards-based grading, which would allow both her and the students to focus more on mastery of key concepts and less upon simply earning a specific grade. The standard-based approach, as Karen came to believe, had a much better chance of focusing students on what mattered most: learning the material.

Karen spent the entire summer rebuilding her assessment plan for the class, and she was excited to test it out during the first semester of the new school year. As she reflected on the summer and her past years of teaching, Karen looked back not only with pride but also with a measure of humility. She was a veteran teacher, and she experienced a deep sadness that some of her past students might have finished her class with a false sense of their abilities based upon a grading system that she now considered unfair. At the same time, she was so happy to have made these new adjustments and looked forward to this new school year.

Reflection and Discussion

1. How would you describe the strengths and weaknesses of Karen's grading and assessment plan during the first part of this story?
2. To what extent do you think that a teacher's approach to grading can impact the success and future vocations or callings of students? Explain.
3. Take a little time to review your own approach to grading and assessment. What do you see as the benefits and limitations? Which students most benefit from your approach? Which students are most disadvantaged by your approach?
4. From a distinctly Christian approach to education, one common understanding is that we are preparing students for a variety of current and future callings or vocations. Not all students will be called to the same things. How might you design grading, feedback, or assessment plans in your classroom that reflect or align with this view of education and vocation?

MAKING A CALL WHEN THE LINES ARE CROSSED

Determining How to Respond as a Mandated Reporter

BY MICHAEL UDEN

If asked to assess her third year of teaching, on most days Jessika Pedersen would rate things as "pretty good." She had more than survived her first two years, even though there had been some rough spots—or, at least, unfamiliar territory—to navigate. Then again, in anyone's first time in a job, don't most things feel a bit unfamiliar?

Jessika accepted a call to All Nations Lutheran School right out of college, and her work as the sixth-grade homeroom and middle-school language arts and visual arts teacher fit her perfectly. When All Nations began as a school in the early 1970s, its West Coast locale was welcoming a wave of immigrants from Asian and Central American countries. Today the neighborhood of All Nations was as globally diverse as ever, but the majority of the school's enrollment was Caucasian, followed by Mexican Americans. This discrepancy was due in part to the plethora of educational alternatives, from for-profit charters to magnet public schools, as well as what many, including Ms. Pedersen, considered a hefty school tuition at All Nations. Being relatively new on the staff, Jessika had learned mostly secondhand of related battles between the school administration and the board of education.

Jessika loved the diversity of her school's neighborhood, even if it was not fully evident at All Nations. Still, diversity was present within her class sections, including socioeconomic and familial diversity. Ms.

Pedersen considered the family names on her first-period class roster, reflecting upon the interactions she had with each so far this school year: David Brandt (single-parent family with a deeply involved mother), Calla Doerscheim (blended family with dad who traveled for work a lot), Javier Ortez (two-parent family who always volunteered), and so on. As Jessika eyed her second-period class list, she also considered which families attended All Nation's association congregations. Of the twenty-eight sixth graders she taught, twelve were members at one of the five association congregations. To Jessika, individual data points such as these did not necessarily matter; however, the composite, that is, the view of the student as a whole person, mattered sometimes more than she could put into words.

"You are studying those class lists a bit too fervently," Marie Schilding joked to Jessika as she entered the sixth-grade homeroom. Marie had retired from the teaching faculty the year before Jessika came, after serving in ministry for nearly all of her forty-three-year career at All Nations. In fact, Jessika assumed Marie's role after the latter's retirement from full-time teaching. While that scenario might strike fear in the heart of most first-year teachers, Jessika's warm and open disposition matched Marie's well. Jessika appreciated Marie's friendship and mentorship, even though she could have been Marie's daughter, if Marie had decided to marry and have children. For her part, Marie was overjoyed to serve as All Nations' part-time resource teacher, as it gave her the chance to work with students (many of whose parents she had also taught) while still providing her more time to read, garden, and paint, three of her favorite pastimes.

"Sorry," Jessika resurfaced from her reflection. "You know I get lost in my thoughts, especially when we are coming back from a school break. I cannot believe they return tomorrow!"

"And the new seating chart?" Marie questioned. "Any new inspiration?"

"When it comes to my beloved sixth graders, especially my dynamic duo, I am feeling less than inspired. I did come up with a new arrangement, though," Jessika shared. Her dynamic duo—David Brandt and Josiah Meyer—had become a challenge shortly after everyone returned from Christmas. For whatever reason—and Jessika had racked her brain to consider any and all possibilities—Josiah had been David's antagonist, though the two hardly appeared to interact at all during the first half of the year. Bullying was the issue, but Jessika's penchant for reflection and deeper consideration was not comfortable relegating the situation entirely to that simple classification.

"I trust David and Josiah are not tablemates," Marie teased, even as she shared Jessika's concern for the situation and had herself attempted to understand more about their dynamic in her resource role.

While any interaction involving people could be considered complicated, especially for the thoughtful and earnest Ms. Pedersen, this situation was even more so. Josiah Meyer, the apparent bully, was the son of a board of education member, and David and his mother, who were not in an association congregation, seemed likely to leave All Nations at the end of the year if things did not improve.

Ms. Pedersen had been mustering all of her resourcefulness to address this schism, even recalling an article about bullying she had read in an "Analysis of Classroom Practice" college course. It struck her, then and now, because it examined bullying from vantage points she had not considered previously. The researchers suggested that bullying in the twenty-first century has been on the rise due to less-established interpersonal skills and coping strategies on the part of children, the vast and often anonymous digital tools of bullies that make the act virtually inescapable, and the fact that the bully has often been a victim of bullying first. Prior to that course, Jessika had never viewed the bully as a possible victim. Her course notes still included a statement her instructor had made at the close of that day's discussion: hurt people hurt people.

Just as she tried whenever there was a classroom conflict, Jessika spent time with David and Josiah—individually and as a pair—to learn more about their relationship and why it had turned. For his part, the shy and reserved David appeared legitimately at a loss as to what had changed from the beginning of the year. Jessika recalled that David and Josiah had even worked as partners in a collaborative art project. David grinned slightly upon recounting that very different interaction and mused, "Josiah seemed like a good guy."

Jessika could make less sense of her conversations with Josiah Meyer. Once emotions had de-escalated, she tried to get her students to move beyond the *what* of a situation to the *why* behind it. During the session, Jessika would ask the students in conflict to reflect on what they were feeling and contrast their emotion at the time of the altercation. While David complied with her request and shared insights such as "I felt betrayed," or "I felt embarrassed," Josiah's feelings were not as apparent. During one conversation, Josiah coolly summarized, "Sometimes people and their feelings don't really matter."

During a later triad conversation with the boys, Jessika began to see the conflict from another vantage point. She asked both boys to offer their explanation as to what had happened to fuel the latest incident. David recounted how he had gone to his locker, only to find all of his things removed and thrown on the floor. Josiah, who stood as tall as Jessika, now sat hunched over in the chair and painfully spoke. "I don't know why a lot of things happen, Ms. Pedersen," he stammered, more as an indictment of his life than a summary of the incident. A humongous tear fell from Josiah's hidden face and saturated his khaki pants. Jessika heard a lot of emotion from him—resignation, frustration, humiliation—but anger seemed at the bottom of the list.

Certainly Ms. Pedersen was not communicating exclusively with David and Josiah. She had been working hard to keep each boy's family aware of the situation as well as her principal, Mr. Dawson. Initially, all of the parents seemed committed to collaborating with her to resolve the situation. Mr. and Mrs. Meyer even specifically thanked Ms. Pedersen as they left the first classroom meeting, indicating appreciation for Jessika's emphasis on open communication and shared resolution. Upon subsequent requests for meetings, however, Mr. Meyer's tone changed. He began to question not only Ms. Pedersen's approach to classroom management but also her overall ability to run an effective classroom. While Jessika had learned on the job how to receive critical feedback without losing her cool or her ground, she was as perplexed by the reaction of her principal, Mr. Dawson. Even though she had briefed him regarding every intervention she was attempting prior to the meetings, he said nothing and simply shook his head back and forth when the Meyers impugned her efforts. Now Jessika was the one who felt bullied, by her principal and by a member of the school board.

Half an hour after the last meeting ended, Ms. Pedersen still sat at her classroom table, reflecting on all that she had experienced that afternoon and her own emotions as well.

"Penny for your thoughts?" Marie's gentle voice broke Jessika's conflicted silence and brought her back to the present.

"It will likely cost you more than a dollar," Jessika quipped. The situation with David and Josiah was feeling like a much larger situation, and she was uneasy.

"Jess, God made us humans with a mind, body, and spirit on purpose," Marie responded. "Consider each of those components as you consider this—whatever it ends up being. Continue to keep everyone informed. And always be faithful in going to our Lord in prayer for all involved."

Jessika smiled sincerely as her mentor exited. As always, Marie was her sage. Ms. Pedersen needed to speak to Mr. Dawson directly.

As she knocked on the frame of his open door, Jessika saw Mr. Dawson studying a spreadsheet of numbers, looking as deep and distant in thought as she had a few minutes earlier. As her principal looked up, his countenance changed, although it was not the change Jessika had hoped to see.

"Come in," he said gruffly, pointing to a chair across from his desk. "I suppose you want to rehash this afternoon's meeting?"

"I want to talk to you about the situation, yes," Jessika tried to stay calm and on the script she had rehearsed in her classroom. "I keep thinking that there is something more to Josiah Meyer's situation—possibly in his home life."

"You mean the home with his dad, who is a member of my board of education? The board that has to approve a budget with a 7 percent increase in spending but no new revenue?" Mr. Dawson continued while holding up the spreadsheet he had been studying as a reference.

"Certainly, I understand that the Meyers are important to All Nations," Jessika acknowledged, "and the Brandts are important too. Still, I am concerned about things Josiah has said. In college, I read an article about bullying that really changed my thinking," Jessika volleyed.

"I read a lot in college too," Mr. Dawson spiked. "This is real life. The situation involving Josiah and David needs to be resolved. Separate them. Monitor them. But do not keep giving detentions. And you cannot continue with meetings in which nothing is settled. People are beginning to question whether this is too much for you," he blasted.

"Thank you for the feedback and direction," Jessika lied as she left his office and exited the building for her car, uncharacteristically without her school bag. Even though her hands were empty, Jessika already had plenty of things with her that needed work.

It is a wonder what a good night of sleep and time in God's Word can do for a person, Jessika thought, as she drove to school the next morning. She entered her classroom bearing a cup of strong coffee for herself and a chai tea thank-you for her confidante, Marie.

In a direct answer to her prayer that morning, the day went smoothly. There was no conflict between David and Josiah, and while Josiah appeared as quiet and reserved as David throughout the afternoon, Ms. Pedersen found herself celebrating the best school day she had experienced in weeks when the final bell rang. Catching up on the grading she had left behind, Jessika was surprised to see Josiah return to her classroom more than an hour after dismissal.

His quiet demeanor of the day was dismissed as well. Josiah Meyer was now darting into her classroom and clearly anxious. She noticed his face wet with tears as he approached her, and he was holding his right arm in a human sling.

"Ms. Pedersen, can I talk to you?" Josiah announced rather than inquired.

"Of course, Josiah. What's going on?" Jessika gently welcomed him.

"I wanted to apologize for yesterday's meeting. My dad said mean things. He says a lot of mean things all the time, but he should not have said that to you," Josiah choked on his words before continuing. "You have always been understanding, even when I treat David badly. I have been thinking a lot about what you said and how I feel. Ms. Pedersen, I know you love me with Christ's love. I want God to forgive me. And I want to tell you. About my dad," as Josiah paused, his body compressed. He was nearly in the fetal position.

"Josiah, what do you want to tell me?" Ms. Pedersen invited.

"Sometimes he gets mad and hurts people, like me." Josiah's tears flowed faster than the words he spoke.

"Give me the words to speak," Jessika prayed as she looked at the trembling boy before her.

"Josiah, it is time to leave." Mr. Meyer stood in her doorway, pronouncing a decree without making eye contact. "Leave your teacher to her work."

Jessika Petersen's mind raced again as she watched Josiah exit. What had happened? What should she do? A flood of recollections came as quickly as Josiah's tears. Mandated reporter. Reasonable person standard. No direct evidence needed, but a need to report directly. Would she inform Mr. Dawson? Should she? What repercussions would her actions have—on herself, on her school?

"Thanks again for the delicious thank-you this morning!" Marie Schilding smiled through the doorway Mr. Meyer had just occupied. The juxtaposition struck Jessika.

"Marie, am I a reasonable person?" Jessika implored.

Marie Schilding quietly made her way to Jessika and embraced her as she sat in the chair Josiah had occupied. While she did not know of his recent conversation, she had seen Mr. Meyer storm out of the building, and she knew both Jessika and the situation well enough to share a story of her own.

"Billy Thomsen," she began, "was a second grader in my second class," she continued. "I was in Missouri then, about your same age. We did not learn much about child abuse in college—times were different—but I knew something was not right for Billy. His eyes were so empty, his heart so heavy. He gave me a Christmas gift and hugged me longer than any other child in the class, as if he was holding on, knowing he might be pulled away."

"What happened to him?" Jessika felt herself in the hug Marie had received decades before.

"He didn't return to school after Christmas. We were told the family moved, although Billy had not mentioned anything about moving. I didn't know what to think at the time, but Billy was always in my thoughts, along with the thought that there was something more I could have done. The next spring, my sister sent me a clipping from the St. Louis newspaper. It was a small story about a young boy killed at the hands of his stepfather. The boy's name was William Thomsen."

"Marie," Jessika grabbed Marie's hand, but Marie retrieved it to wipe her tears.

"I've never forgotten that article or that boy or that feeling I had all along," Marie confessed. "You are one of the most reasonable people I know, Jessika Pedersen. Be faithful in going to our Lord for all involved," Marie concluded, embracing Jessika's hand.

Reflection and Discussion

The effects of sin in our world run deep and cause serious damage to many. Yet we have a Savior who rescues us from our sinful condition. Read and reflect on the following Scripture passages and how they apply to the issues presented in this chapter: Mark 9:42; Mark 10:14; Romans 13:8–10; Romans 8:1–2.

1. If Jessika Pedersen shares her concerns about her student Josiah Meyer with her school administrator, will she have met her obligation as a mandated reporter?
2. A "reasonable person standard" applies in mandated reporting, meaning the consideration is whether a reasonable person, if confronted with the same situation, would find the child at risk for abuse or neglect. Do you feel that standard was met in this case study? Why or why not?
3. Mr. Dawson, the school principal, is attempting to manage many elements simultaneously and, as a result, may not be performing proficiently. What direction might you give him?
4. Research indicates that bullying is becoming more common in schools. How do you address bullying in your classroom?

A YOUNG WRITER AND A LEARNER-EMPOWERING TEACHER

BY BERNARD BULL

Ever since she first picked up a crayon, Jenny loved to write. Before she knew the alphabet, she scribbled symbols on a page and took pride in reading her imaginary books to anyone who would listen. Sometimes she wrote extravagant tales of princesses and dragons. Other times she wrote innovative news about what the neighbor kids did in the backyard yesterday. As she got older and learned how to read, she read anything she could find. Then she tried to write something similar.

Nobody knew why she loved to write. None of her family members were writers, and none could recall any formative experiences about writing. It just clicked for her. It wasn't that she was an especially good writer, at least not yet. She just had this love for it. She enjoyed it even if others didn't seem interested in what she wrote. She wrote with or without the praise and recognition of others.

Every day, Jenny woke up and reached for the notebook in which she would try to remember her dreams, using part of one as a spark for a new short story. On most mornings, she sat in bed until she finished writing it. Then she would head to breakfast and off to school. At night, she pulled out her laptop and wrote some more, often writing until she fell asleep or her parents told her to turn off the laptop.

This was the life of Jenny the writer, and she did call herself that. If you ever had the pleasure to meet her, she would shake your hand and, with the confidence of a CEO, say, "Hi, I'm Jenny and I'm a writer." She didn't say that she wanted to be a writer. She didn't say she set the goal of becoming a writer. She explained that she was a writer. From her viewpoint, a writer is someone who writes, and they do it often, even every day. She certainly fit that description, and she was proud to call herself that.

If you asked her about what she planned to do with her writing, she usually wouldn't answer in the way many people expected. They wanted her to explain how she would use writing for a career in the future, but Jenny didn't think about careers. She just thought about writing. She always answered their question by listing off the many current and future writing projects on her mental agenda. The goal was not to publish a bestseller or get an article in a top magazine. Jenny cared more about getting the words on paper (or the digital equivalent) and sharing what she wrote with other people, even if nobody chose to read it.

Something important happened during her tenth-grade year, a wonderful something. It was the first full day of the school year, and Jenny sat in the cafeteria, writing in her notebook. It wasn't that she didn't have any friends or didn't want to be around them. On the contrary; she had plenty of good friends. It was just that she had an idea and had to get it on paper. Her closest friends knew this and respected her for it.

After lunch, Jenny attended the class that she had anticipated all summer. It was a new English class, and she couldn't wait to meet the teacher and use this class as a chance to learn more about writing. When she arrived to class and received the syllabus, she acted a bit like she just got a full list of her upcoming Christmas presents. She read through it carefully, noting the books and essays for the class, many of which she had read in the past. Then she read about the various writing assignments. She was disappointed that there wasn't more writing in the course, and she debated with herself about talking to the teacher.

The school had a gifted program, but it was not an option for Jenny because she didn't meet the formal criteria. She didn't have a high GPA or any high standardized test scores that her school used to qualify students for the program. She wasn't a documented genius, as some might measure it. She was just deeply curious and loved to write. That passion pushed her to increasingly greater levels of knowledge and skill in this area.

Jenny tended to be on the shy side, but when it came to her love of writing, she was willing to speak up. So, she did just that. After class, she asked the teacher, Ms. Bentley, if she could talk to her. She explained her love of writing, something she didn't really have to explain. Her last teacher had already prepared Ms. Bentley for Jenny entering the class. Then she explained, "I'm very excited about many of the wonderful readings that we have in the class, but I was also really hoping to focus more on writing."

Ms. Bentley did something that Jenny had never experienced before in school. She thanked Jenny for her comments and asked if she would be willing to be her writing consultant for the year. Not sure what her teacher meant, Jenny asked for more details. As Ms. Bentley described it, the writing consultant would play the role of making sure that three key writing outcomes were achieved during the semester. First, she wanted to create the best possible chance of helping more students discover the love of writing. Second, the writing consultant had the charge of making sure that every single student in the class saw the value of becoming a good writer. Third, she wanted Jenny to help make sure that every student in the class understood how writing could be used to have a significant and lasting impact in the world.

Jenny couldn't believe what she was hearing. This was a dream for her. While it wasn't exactly the writing workshop that she initially wanted, she embraced the chance to take on this role and be a champion for something so important to her.

Jenny accepted the challenge and went to work that night. She brainstormed all the different possible ways to meet these three goals. She headed to the library and asked the librarian to help her find articles and information that might help with the challenge. She went online and located some writers' forums on which she shared the assignment and asked for ideas. Before long, Jenny had a long list of possibilities, far more than would be possible to include. She continued to get feedback from others, including Ms. Bentley, until she narrowed down the plan to a few key ideas followed by a dozen smaller projects.

Even as she started to create a plan, word got out about this experiment though social media and the writers' forums online. Before long, Jenny had published authors reaching out to her, offering to help. That inspired her to reach out directly to others. Within a week, Jenny had a lineup of five different published authors and journalists ready to serve as "author of the week." On the first day of the week, the author agreed to join the class live for a fifteen-minute virtual introduction along with a short question-and-answer period. She worked with Ms. Bentley to include something related to the author each week, giving students a little exposure to this author's life and work. As a fun tie-in, they managed to plan it so that the author of the week aligned with a short story or novel that was personally meaningful to that author. Then, they would finish the week with a second, follow-up live session. In other words, Jenny managed to get fifteen professional authors and writers to join the class over the year, each one sharing stories of how writing affected their lives and how they used writing to impact the lives of others.

This was just the beginning. Jenny launched a writing competition in the class and found local organizations (and one national publisher) that were willing to give money or other prizes for the winners. Each writing competition focused on challenging students to "do good through writing" and submit their entry. Entries could be letters to the editor, blog posts, short stories, articles in the local newspaper or somewhere else, or any other creative effort as long as the writing was shared with a public audience. Because not all students had the confidence to participate at first, she started an after-school writing group to help people with their writing competition projects.

Others in the school heard about the writing group, and these writing competitions were picked up by all the sophomore English classes. Her after-school writing group grew from three to almost twenty by the end of the semester. Jenny had no idea that so many classmates shared her interest in writing. It just took a little encouragement to take some risks in this area.

Jenny earned mostly Bs that semester, with a B+ in sophomore English, yet she had the single most amazing experience of all her years in school. She built a network with authors and journalists. She had new confidence in her abilities as a leader. She was even more passionate about being a writer, and she helped others discover the value of writing in life. She learned more about writing, including the real-world business of being a writer, in that one semester than in her whole life previously. Not only that, but her work as a writing consultant left a permanent mark on the culture of the school, the writing lives of countless students, and how the English faculty went about teaching writing for years to come.

Reflection and Discussion

1. Jenny's passion was for writing, but every student has some pursuits that inspire and excite them. Scan the roster of students in one or more of your classes. Can you list each of their main passions and interests? If not, how might you learn more about them?
2. How do you or how might you tap into the passions and interests of individual students in your class or in school?
3. One potential lesson from this story is the power of personalized or individualized challenges and projects based upon student's passions and interest. Looking at your list of students and their passions, take a few minutes to brainstorm ideas of personalized challenges that you might offer to a few of those students.
4. Read 1 Corinthians 12:21–31. From our Christian perspective and based on this Scripture passage, we recognize that people have different gifts and different callings. How is your classroom and school designed to recognize and celebrate this reality?

HONORS NIGHT

BY JIM PINGEL

"Tonight we honor and give recognition to the many gifts and talents our heavenly Father has so abundantly given to our students," Principal Rachel Jefferson told a packed gymnasium at Trinity Lutheran School on a Thursday night in May. "You know," she continued, "our community has one newspaper, made up of two parts—the front page and the sports page. Now don't get me wrong—I love our sports programs and students' athletic accomplishments," she insisted. "But sports teams and individual athletes get their names printed in the paper or posted on blogs almost every day. And that's wonderful," she asserted. "But I think that it's time that we take even just one night a year to recognize formally our students' academic, musical, artistic, and other achievements too. So thank you for being here tonight as we honor the many and various God-given gifts and talents of our students in a special way."

A first-year principal not yet thirty years old, but wise beyond her years, Jefferson made her point: there are other student achievements and blessings to celebrate besides athletic accomplishments. Outspoken on the issue, Jefferson understood that she risked agitating the athletic Goliath. Trinity's sports programs, after all, excelled in so many areas, particularly in volleyball and basketball. Almost every other year, the seventh- and eighth-grade girls' and boys' basketball teams dominated the area and advanced to compete in the state and national tournaments. The local public and Lutheran high school coaches frequently attended Trinity Tiger volleyball games hoping to recruit the star athletes to their respective schools. Individual cross-country runners excelled annually in competitions and races with other local public and private school runners. The local newspaper, blogs, and YouTube videos featured stories, sometimes even short documentaries, on Trinity's student athletes and various athletic accomplishments. If you heard about Trinity Lutheran School in the community, you probably heard about the school in the context of a top-notch sports program.

Jefferson was herself an avid fitness enthusiast and recreational swimmer, and she loved sports and athletic competitions. Few of her faculty and staff knew that she had once been a decorated, three-sport athlete in high school (volleyball, basketball, and soccer) before tearing her ACL during her senior basketball season (after which three prominent Division 1 NCAA schools withdrew their soccer scholarship offers to her). Moreover, she treasured the positive press that Trinity's athletic successes brought to their school of 235 students (Pre-K through eighth grade). Good publicity is always helpful for student recruitment.

During her first year at Trinity, however, as she tried to listen to the school community and learn about her new school's culture, certain observations bothered her. Why was it that sports team scores or individual athletic accomplishments were always reported or shared in the morning announcements, but not any academic, music, or other non-athletic accomplishments? The school's website and social media feeds were filled with athletic highlights, student-athlete interviews captured on YouTube, and statements on the big upcoming match or game. As she reviewed past issues of the school's monthly electronic newsletter, *Tiger Times*, she noted that athletes who received first-team or second-team designations in their middle school conference were prominently featured with pictures, quotes, and their favorite things listed. After each season ended, sports team banquets took place at local area restaurants, often accompanied by big-name community guest speakers. Jefferson wondered where they got the money for these events and speakers.

While publicity on athletics permeated their literature and communication streams, Jefferson found very few features on band, choir, art, forensics, student council, robotics, or STEM students. Academic achievements were rarely mentioned or publicized, though there were notices for the annual Christmas concert in the December *Tiger Times* issue. At first, she wondered if Trinity's academics were subpar or if their music program lacked leadership or direction. As the weeks went by, however, she realized these contemplations were wrong. Jefferson questioned why the volleyball and basketball teams were on a two-year budget cycle for receiving new uniforms, while the forensics and drama teams had to do their own fundraising for transportation and new microphones, and the computer lab was filled with machines over seven years old. She also noticed that student-athletes were often excused at two o'clock and missed seventh- and eighth-hour class multiple times in order to travel to nonconference and conference competitions. Why didn't the previous principal change the schedule to make sure those hours or classes were not always the same ones students missed? The fact that Trinity planned to build a new practice gym so that student athletes would not have to practice so late into the evening also puzzled her. Certainly, she understood that demand for gym space and practice time were at a premium, but music students still had no band or choir room to use on a daily basis and had to rehearse in the cafeteria or the church sanctuary, whichever happened to be available at the time. Jefferson also noted that in the proposed practice gym, one wing would have an athletic hall of fame. Who had ever heard of an athletic hall of fame to recognize middle schoolers? After further inquiry, Jefferson discovered that some leading Trinity members wanted to induct star student athletes of the past potentially to increase their alumni and third-source gifting, but also because, well, the sports people thought it would be a cool idea. One thing stood out to the new, young principal: the Trinity community sure cared a lot about their athletes and sports program.

So in her inaugural year as principal, Jefferson deviated from her decision to spend the first year listening and learning rather than making big changes. She installed the newly dubbed "Honors Night." God was calling on her to balance out the co-curricular programs. The focus would be on lifting up student achievement and accomplishments in academics, scholarship, the arts, and Christian servant leadership. Most importantly, the evening would provide yet another platform to witness and share Christ and all of His blessings. Unfortunately, the only person Jefferson vetted this idea with was herself.

After presenting the conceptual design of Honors Night to her faculty in a February faculty meeting, the rookie administrator was stunned to receive so little enthusiasm and even some backlash about her concept. Some on the faculty chaffed at any kind of awards night in general, claiming that it smacked of exalting works righteousness. How could they really honor someone for servant leadership? How could anyone really know what is in someone's heart? We don't serve God to get an award, they railed. Give out a theology department award? Does that mean we are indicating that some students are more righteous and holy than others, that they obeyed the Ten Commandments better than others?

Initially, Jefferson thought their arguments were very Pharisaic and selectively judgmental. Hadn't they noticed that there were awards and rewards for almost everything in society and for so many other things at Trinity? Did they object to the conference championship banners hanging in the gym, the sports team awards given out on banquet nights, or the scholarships awarded to eighth-grade students so they could attend the local Lutheran high school? Were they against the Super Bowl trophy too? Jefferson pondered these things in her heart. Maybe they had a point. Perhaps she was being too sentimental, too warm-and-fuzzy toward the students God placed under her care.

Other teachers inquired if there would be any sports awards given. "I've been thinking about that," Jefferson responded, having anticipated the question. "You all already do your own banquet, end-of-season awards ceremonies with MVP, Most Improved, Hustle Award, and so on. And our student athletes already get recognized for all-conference awards." Demonstrating command of the athletic arena, Jefferson continued, "But do you give out any kind of Christian athlete of the year award or Christian servant leadership award?" A few coaches smirked. "This rookie principal wants me to give something nice to the water boy or water girl on my team," one joked. "Well, what would be wrong with that if he or she is deserving?" Jefferson retorted as she overheard the conversation. "Doesn't Scripture tell us that God chose the lowly, weak, and foolish to do His bidding and shame the wise?" Having paraphrased one of her favorite passages in Scripture (1 Corinthians 1:26–31), Jefferson quickly reigned in her emotions. "I'm just saying, why not look at different ways to affirm and recognize our students for the different and wonderful gifts God has given to them?"

Some faculty members carefully and earnestly wondered out loud if Jefferson's proposal was akin to giving everyone a blue ribbon for living. "I understand and think I even support what you are trying to do, Rachel," said one of the teachers. "I just don't want us to water down excellence or hand out participation certificates and stickers to everyone just to keep parents happy."

"That's a fair enough concern," said Jefferson. "But I'm not proposing that everyone gets a trophy. I simply want kids to be acknowledged and encouraged in their God-given gifts." She paused deliberately. "And perhaps just as importantly, I want all of us to make sure we are looking and helping students identify just how special God made them and how special they are in His eyes."

There were a few faculty members, mostly ones who saw the sports machine dominate the other agencies and programs of the school, who supported Jefferson's proposal. Nonetheless, the truth was that most faculty members were tired. Displaying some of her inexperience, Jefferson had rolled out her Honors Day proposal in February—during the dog days of a school year. Adding one more thing on one more night seemed like an unnecessary burden to bear. "My fellow colleagues," Jefferson lowered her voice after twenty-five minutes of discussion back on that February morning meeting, "I'm asking you to pray about this and to give it your best shot. Why not try it? Everything sports-oriented in this community and in our school gets all the love and praise. Why not lift up some other things too—arguably more important things, which will make much more of an impact in the long run?" She made her final closing argument: "I wouldn't be proposing this if I didn't think it could enhance our ministry, lift up our students, and give glory to God." Then she added shrewdly, "If it goes badly, I'll take the heat. After all, I'm new and don't know how things are supposed to go around here. But if it goes well, then I thank you all in advance for helping to make it happen. Will you join me in prayer about this and ask God to bless our efforts?"

After her opening remarks at the start of Honors Night, Principal Jefferson had one of the star eighth-grade volleyball players give a short opening devotion and prayer. Few people had seen such a prominent athlete lead a devotion on her own.

Scholarship awards were next on the evening agenda. Out of the twenty-five eighth graders graduating from Trinity, twenty-one would be attending the local Lutheran high school, an all-time high in terms of a percentage of the class (84 percent). Thanks to a few supportive donors and some shrewd marketing by the executive director of the Lutheran high school, ten Trinity students would be receiving $2,500 scholarships. Five of the scholarship winners would be based on merit (they had to write a short essay and be interviewed by three teachers of the Lutheran high school). Five others would be selected, based on financial need, by Principal Jefferson.

Lutheran high school executive director, Dr. Al Zimmer, not only announced the recipients of the five merit-based scholarship winners but also asked these five students to read their essays in front of the evening audience. The essay asked students to write about the faith lessons they learned while attending Trinity Lutheran School. One by one, the students went up to the podium to speak. The first young lady talked about her struggle in dealing with diminished playing time on the basketball team. Angry at first and humbled throughout the ordeal, she spoke eloquently about God's plans for her life, the call to be more empathetic to others, and how her struggle helped her to become a more patient and compassionate teammate toward others. The next student commented on the most important thing he learned from each of his teachers while at Trinity. He had the crowd rolling in laughter as he roasted his beloved teachers on their idiosyncrasies and quirky ways. Yet another student lifted up his single mom and all that she had sacrificed to make his education possible at Trinity. The next young lady articulated her passion for music and how she hoped to glorify God with her musical talents and voice. She closed her short speech by singing a verse from the song "In Christ Alone." The final student recalled the suicide of his father during his fourth-grade year, and how the teachers and congregational members rose up to support him and his baby sister when they needed it most. All of the students' readings were deeply personal and moving. Parents and grandparents alike reached often for tissues to dab their eyes.

One by one, teachers came up next to give departmental awards to deserving sixth-, seventh-, and eighth-grade students. In addition to the eighth graders, Jefferson wanted academic, arts, and service awards to be given to sixth- and seventh-grade students as well. To see eighth graders receive scholarships and recognition for Christian servant leadership, as well as hearing their personal and deeply moving speeches, would certainly make an impression on the younger students and their parents. Indeed, these sixth and seventh graders would soon be the eighth grade leaders of Trinity. In her attempt to lift up and build the academic, art, and servant leadership culture of her school, Jefferson was intentionally playing the long game.

As Honors Night proceeded to unfold, Principal Jefferson listened, observed, and took notes:

- The math department chair gave the math award to the student who did things "faster and quicker" than anyone else—just like this student did on the volleyball court! The analogy fit, Jefferson grudgingly admitted, but even here at an academic awards night, *we still cannot escape the athletic beast.*
- The English department chair gave the award to the top English student, but added that what separated this student from all the rest was the way she integrated Scripture in almost all of her writing assignments. *Yes,* thought Jefferson, *someone bringing the mission statement alive in an organic way here on Honors Night. Well done!*
- The social studies chair gave the department award to the student who not only did good work but also demonstrated a love for history. Jefferson applauded the decision, but anticipated a call from a parent whose child had a higher percentage grade. She quickly made a notation: *Did we define criteria for "love of history"?*
- The technology teacher gave the department award to the student who hung out in his lab every day after school. *Deserving, or teacher's pet? What criteria were used?*
- One of Trinity's pastors came up to give the theology department award to a Catholic student. *Not sure if Pastor knows this girl is Catholic. I'm okay with it, but is he?*
- The science department chair gave the science award to a student who was not only one of the top students in class but also exhibited servant leadership in the lab portions of class. *Love it! Ask how you measure or assess servant leadership in lab.*

- The art department chair gave the art award to the student who showed the most improvement over the course of the semester. *Wow. Bold. Improvement focused. Growth mindset—yes! What criteria were used?*
- The athletic director gave the awards for male and female Christian athletes of the year to Trinity's two most decorated athletes. *Expected. Boring. No mention of Christian attributes or servant leadership. Criteria?*
- The drama/musical director gave the drama award to "not a Peter but an Andrew, someone who works behind the scenes and stage, someone who serves others so that the show must go on." *Very cool. Not an athlete or even a main performer, but still a star.*
- Eight eighth-grade students were called up to receive servant leadership awards (and one-hundred-dollar gift cards) as nominated and voted upon by the faculty and staff of Trinity. The school secretary and Principal Jefferson presented the awards and read comments given by teachers and staff members on why these particular students were receiving recognition. *It felt good to recognize some kids who don't normally get recognized.*

As one of the drama students closed the evening in prayer, she recited the school's mission statement, ". . . and thank You, God, for giving us Trinity Lutheran School—a school that, by God's grace, inspires each of us to love You with all our heart, all our soul, and all our mind."

The first annual Honors Night was history. Rachel Jefferson knew her inbox would be busy during the next twenty-four hours. She had work to do.

Reflection and Discussion

Read the following Bible passages and use them as the basis to begin your discussion of this chapter: Matthew 5:16; Matthew 25:21; Colossians 3:23–24; James 1:12; 1 Corinthians 1:26–31; Proverbs 3:27.

1. How should Christian teachers honor and praise their students? How and in what ways should schools recognize students? What do you do in your context?
2. Evaluate Rachel Jefferson's job performance and Honors Night initiative. One challenge first-year principals or administrators have is of knowing when or how fast to make changes (if changes are even necessary at all). What did she do well and not so well?
3. Analyze what you and your school recognize, laud, or highlight. How big a role does sports, or any other co-curricular, play in your school? Do they overshadow your academic emphasis and programs? What message are you sending to your students, parents, and the community about what you value and honor?
4. How do you feel about rewarding or recognizing students for service and faith development? Why?
5. What stood out to you about the actual Honors Night? What did you like? What did you dislike? What would you have done differently?

AN UNCONVENTIONAL TEACHER IN A CONVENTIONAL SYSTEM

BY BERNARD BULL

Nea loved teaching. More accurately, she loved helping and watching students learn. The more confident and curious the students became, the more fulfilled she felt. Far from your common idea of a teacher standing in the front of the room conducting a neat and tidy orchestra of learners, Nea's class was a blend of messy and focused, organic and calculated, curious and driven. Students worked alone, in teams, laughed, collaborated, and largely managed their own schedule apart from a few group checkpoints each day. Students were curious and loved to learn, at least most of the time.

Of course, like every classroom, students didn't always come to class ready and anxious to learn. They brought with them the fears and anxieties of early adolescence. They brought family squabbles and tensions with them. The joys and tensions of finding their place among peers certainly came along to each class session as well. Nonetheless, most days Nea found effective ways to direct her students' attention toward a compelling problem, question, lesson, or learning activity.

Each day, Nea woke up excited for another day of school, as did many of her students. While many teachers worried about preparing students for the next test, increasing expectations around covering the common core standards, and abundant regulations, Nea didn't pay much attention to these. When they fit and made sense, she found a way to include them. Long ago, she resolved never to let tests, regulations, and standards get in the way of creating a rich and engaging culture of learning for her students. She came to school, welcomed the students, opened class with a time of prayer and devotions, closed the door, and did her own thing. Or, rather, they (she and the students) did their own thing. The class did not belong to Nea, not as she thought of the classroom. Instead, she saw herself as a guide, while the students grew in self-assurance and gradually (sometimes it took a full semester) increased in their ability to take greater ownership in what and how they learned.

All around her, teachers taught and ran their classes more traditionally. They managed their classes. They set rules. They prepped students for tests and aligned what they did with the necessary state and national standards. Nea didn't do any of these, at least not in the way others did. She did not explicitly break rules, nor did she invest extra time in protesting established standards and policies that clashed with her classroom culture. She just didn't seem to pay much attention to them. She believed that what she and her students were doing was important, that it worked, and that students valued it. That was enough for her.

While most students loved her class and looked forward to it daily, not everyone shared this enthusiasm. Several teachers derided Nea's extreme practices and wondered why the principal didn't crack down on what they considered a blatant disregard for standard policy and practice. Most parents loved what was happening in Nea's class, but a few outspoken parents did not. They disliked the fact that Nea didn't use or give traditional grades. They wanted something that resembled their school experience, and they worried that her unorthodox approach would leave their children ill-prepared for the next level of school, not to mention decreasing their performance on state testing. For them, getting high grades and high test scores was an important sign of success in school, and they wanted that for their children.

Nea knew that people thought these things about her, but she didn't pay much attention to it. She exuded an unusual confidence in the path that she had chosen for herself and her students, and she stood ready to describe and defend it to anyone who might ask. She knew that she was disregarding school policy and standard practice, but for Nea, there were just some things that were more important than policies. Nea reasoned that if students were learning and growing in their faith, and if she was being faithful to the school mission, then she was fulfilling her calling as a teacher. Not everyone agreed with this line of thinking.

Murmurs of dissatisfaction from a few parents and other teachers made their way to the principal. The principal knew about what Nea did in her class. He knew that it didn't comply with some of the school policies and standard classroom practice, but Nea's students had actually performed quite well on the last set of standardized tests. For some reason, this wasn't enough for a few parents, and they voiced their strong concern, demanding that the principal do something about this rogue teacher. They amplified their voice by talking directly to a number of school board members who, in return, passed their concern back to the superintendent, and through her, back to the principal. The superintendent didn't say much except to make it clear that she expected the principal to address the issue: "Do something about this."

The principal didn't see himself as having much of a choice. He set up a meeting with Nea. He expressed the concerns that he heard, noting the pressure he was getting from the superintendent and others. "What you do with the students is wonderful. Students love going to class. They are learning. They take ownership in their learning. However, people are just not ready for this. I need you to get your class back into line with more conventional approaches to teaching."

Nea listened politely. She didn't show much emotion. She calmly asked if she could take a couple of days to process what she had just heard. "I need a little time to think about what you just told me and what it means for me and my students." The principal agreed. It was Friday, so the principal scheduled a follow-up meeting for the next Tuesday afternoon. Nea left the office. She was quiet, contemplative, and seemingly curious, as if she were trying to solve some complex puzzle.

Returning to her class, even as she pondered this comment from the principal, Nea continued with her unconventional and student-centered teaching. She wandered the class, affirming students as they worked alone and in teams. She offered suggestions and used probing questions to guide them. Nea was proud of the classroom and community that she had created. "This is what real teaching is all about," she thought to herself. As the bell rang and students departed, she watched them, smiling but with a few tears welling up in her eyes. "How could I possibly stop doing this?" Nea left school that day deep in thought about what to do. It was a three-day weekend, so she had some extra time to think and pray about her next steps.

On Tuesday morning, Nea arrived in her classroom and started activities just as she did on every other week. Students arrived excited, curious, and ready to take ownership for their learning that week. She smiled, encouraged, and asked questions to guide students when needed. She drew them together for the morning and mid-morning devotion and listened as students shared their challenges and joys of various class projects. She was happy, and so were they.

Then came the time for her afternoon meeting with the principal. They greeted each other, sat down, and didn't say anything for what seemed like a full minute. Nea broke the silence.

"Thank you for giving me a few days to process our discussion from last Friday. I understand that you are in a difficult position. I've been grateful for the leeway that you've given me over the past years in my classroom, and I hope you know that, in doing so, you are part of the rich and engaging learning community that gathers in my classroom each day. You've visited my classroom enough to know what it is like. Students are engaged, enthusiastic, curious, and making impressive strides in their learning across many fields. It is a joy to watch them grow in confidence and take ownership for their learning. So, I just want to thank you for helping to make that happen over these past years."

She continued, "It would be dishonest for me to claim that I am not disappointed, even saddened, by our conversation last week and by the complaints that you are receiving. I've been thinking about this problem for the last few days, and I can't, in good conscience, simply do what other teachers are doing in the school. I learned from a wise theologian that it is neither good nor wise to go against one's conscience. When our actions and convictions are in conflict, bad things tend to follow. I am not a teacher. I've never been called just to teach in the traditional sense. I am far more interested in designing experiences and creating contexts in which students learn, and that no longer seems to be a welcome approach in this school. As such, I offer you my letter of resignation today. I am happy to stay on as long as you deem it useful and appropriate."

The principal was visibly disappointed and expressed as much. He valued Nea and what she brought to the school, but he didn't know any way around this challenge. They talked through the situation a bit more and then decided together that Nea would finish the school year, but move on from there. The rest of the school year went well, and Nea left the school on good terms with the principal and others in the community. Most people would describe the situation as one in which Nea was just not a good fit for the school, and that she was better off finding a school that more closely aligned with her approach to teaching and learning.

Reflection and Discussion

1. To what extent do you relate to the challenge of Nea? Do you ever find yourself compelled to just "close the door and do your thing" as it relates to teaching?
2. Can you think of anything that Nea could have done proactively to address questions and concerns about some of her more unconventional classroom practices?
3. As you consider the Fourth Commandment and the greater counsel of Scripture, what advice would you give to a teacher such as Nea? What advice might you give to the principal?
4. To what extent do you deem this a positive outcome of the situation? Can you think of other or better potential outcomes?
5. What advice might you give to a teacher who finds himself or herself constrained by existing school policies and practices?

TEXTBOOK SCIENCE RECONSIDERED

BY BERNARD BULL

James wanted to be a scientist one day, so he was excited to start school and learn as much as possible. As a sixth grader, this was his first experience in a traditional Christian school. Prior to this year, he had been homeschooled, and he immersed himself in science daily through kitchen lab experiments and a rich environmental education curriculum hosted by a local nature preserve. There he spent six hours a week out in nature, learning about science as he experienced the natural world. In addition to this, his parents taught him to set up simple scientific experiments to explore things that interested him. As a sixth grader, he'd already learned to create and conduct basic experiments in psychology, basic chemistry, biology, and earth science. When James thought of science, he thought of doing things, conducting experiments, and using the scientific method.

In addition, James saw science as an opportunity to explore the wonders of God's creation. "The heavens declare the glory of God, and the sky above proclaims His handiwork" (Psalm 19:1). Science evoked a sense of awe and wonder. Going on a hike through the nearby woods, identifying plants and types of trees, and simply enjoying the beauty of nature—these all connected to James's idea of science.

When he arrived in science class for the first time, James was confused when the first weeks consisted of working through a textbook and associated worksheets. In fact, science class continued that way for the first six weeks. Not until the seventh week did the class even have a chance to conduct their first experiment, and it seemed like the teacher was far more interested in how they filled out a provided worksheet than conducting what he thought of as an actual experiment.

James hoped that this was just how they started science each year. He thought that maybe the teacher needed to help people learn some basic vocabulary and facts to get ready for the real work of science. Yet the semester continued, and so did the focus on multiple-choice and matching tests and quizzes, worksheets, reading chapter after chapter without experiencing the concepts in any real way, and learning about science facts instead of doing science.

James still loved science, at least the way that he'd come to think of it in the past, but this new classroom-based experience left him disappointed and increasingly disinterested. A subject that previously fascinated him and had him spending hours experimenting and thinking about increasingly complex concepts was now something that he started to dread each day. It was a bit like coming back from a several-year safari and now being told that reading a textbook about a safari was supposed to be superior somehow. James didn't buy it. He had experienced the joy of science, and he knew that what they were doing in class was far from that reality. He knew that the grandeur of God's creation far exceeded the glossy pictures and charts in his science book.

One day during lunch, James was explaining his struggle and disappointment to a couple of classmates. None of them had the rich experience of James as a student, but they were curious. They also thought it was amazing that he actually got to conduct so many experiments in the past, and that he had a chance to do hands-on learning activities. They all agreed that what James described would make for a far more interesting course.

At the same time, James didn't realize that his science teacher was on lunch duty that day and was standing nearby, close enough to hear pretty much everything that he just said. As Mr. Baxter listened, he couldn't help but be saddened by what he heard. He didn't disagree with anything that James shared. What James described in his early experiences was the very part of science that once led Mr. Baxter to become a biology major in college. Yet listening to James helped Mr. Baxter realize that his class didn't resemble any of that.

Mr. Baxter went home that night and thought more about what he heard. He wondered how he managed to let his class go so far astray from actually doing science and from helping students experience the incredible beauty of God's creation. Somewhere along the way, he just got caught up in the business of the day and the tyranny of the urgent. He managed to confuse teaching about science with teaching people to think scientifically and to experience the joy and wonder of God's world.

Inspired by that simple, serendipitous moment in the lunchroom, Mr. Baxter decided that it was time for a classroom makeover. He wasn't ready to throw out the textbook or the importance of learning scientific facts. He thought it was important to make sure that students had the guidance and the direct instruction that he considered important when learning certain scientific concepts. At the same time, he was going to make it a personal mission to help students learn the joy of experiencing and doing science. As such, he made it a goal of creating at least two rich and engaging hands-on learning experiences each week. For one of those two, students would have the challenge and opportunity to think and behave like scientists by conducting experiments and even learning to set up their own.

It took him a few weeks to get things organized. After that, Mr. Baxter's makeover was complete and he was ready to give it a try. It wasn't an easy transition for some students. In fact, some of the straight-A kids were not sure about all these changes. A few even complained to their parents, who in return complained to the principal. Nevertheless, when Mr. Baxter explained to the principal what he was doing, he had the administrator's full support and encouragement.

It took some students a couple months to make the transition from the old way of thinking about science to this new one. However, eventually most of the class joined in the fun. What was previously a good, orderly, and interesting class now began to take on a completely different energy. Students became a little more inquisitive. They seemed to take a greater sense of pride in their work. Anyone passing by would hear and see a buzz in the class as students worked together on experiments and commented on their growing number of hands-on experiences. Students used expressions of awe and wonder, and Mr. Baxter used each of those to remind students about the God who makes all of this possible. In addition to this, Mr. Baxter's love for teaching and science shifted to an all-time high.

For James, this was more like it. In fact, he couldn't have been happier going to class each day. This was the science that he knew and loved.

Reflection and Discussion

1. Sometimes teachers learn their most important lessons from the students. What lessons do students teach you?
2. Whether you teach science or music, English or history, there are ample opportunities to point out God's role in your field. How do you help students experience the joy or wonder in one or more of the subjects that you teach?
3. While the common features of a class such as tests and textbooks are not bad, they often do not succeed in helping students experience the full wonder and joy of a subject or topic. How do you help students discover the true wonder or joy of what you are teaching?

DIVERSITY TRAINING

BY JIM PINGEL

Workshop: Morning Session

Principal Steven Jameson was nervous. Last year, Immanuel Lutheran Church and School joined the new state voucher program. This meant that twenty-five new students, formerly enrolled in (mostly) urban public schools, would be joining the Immanuel Lutheran Pioneer K–8 family. Most of these new students would be students of color. The influx of voucher students would increase the school's enrollment to 175 students and provide yet another opportunity to share the Gospel and teach the faith to unchurched families. All of these prospects excited Jameson. His anxiety, however, centered on the concerns many of his longtime faculty members expressed to him privately: Are we bringing in some, you know, bad apples that might ruin the special school climate we've established? What do we really know about these kids and their families anyway? Are we really trained or prepared to handle these kinds of students? Would the new students actually hurt enrollment in the long run? Since Immanuel has high academic standards and sends our graduates to elite high schools, will these new students be able to keep up, or will they hinder teachers from maintaining high curriculum standards and expectations? How many more voucher students are we planning to take next year anyway? What's the vision or plan?

Jameson listened patiently to these questions and concerns. While he did not believe these faculty members were racist or carried racist views, their questions agitated him nonetheless. Perhaps, however, their viewpoints were his fault. After all, Immanuel faculty and staff had never gone through any culturally responsive training, and most came from lily-white upbringings and backgrounds. This was not their fault, of course, but Jameson felt he needed to broaden their ministry perspective and open their hearts and minds to the new mission field that God had now brought to Immanuel.

Jameson was actually kicking himself for not orchestrating some kind of diversity training before the acceptance of the voucher program anyway. His school had already realized changes in the student body makeup, especially in regard to diversity of ethnicity, socioeconomic background, and religion. For the last decade, their city's demographics had seen significant changes, like many other regions throughout the country. Families of color now made up the majority of the city's population. Some white flight had taken place as many generational families moved to the suburbs where new, affluent jobs in high-tech and health care industries were flourishing. Furthermore, no matter the demographic group—black, white, Latino, Asian, or any other—families continued to splinter and suffer as divorce rates and out-of-wedlock birth rates increased. The opioid epidemic and widespread acceptance of pot and marijuana use only complicated the challenges confronting students, working-class families, and Immanuel Lutheran School. Satan sure knew what he was doing, Jameson thought, to attack the family unit with deadly precision.

While the demographics of the students and families had changed at Immanuel, the faculty and staff had not. All of the teachers and support staff were white, except for Marianna Lopez, their outstanding Spanish instructor who served grades 4 through 8 (and taught the physical education classes too). A devout Catholic, Marianna loved teaching at Immanuel and connected students to God's Word better than almost any other teacher. Her fourth- and second-grade daughters attended Immanuel and loved the school. Since there were not a whole lot of competent Lutheran Spanish teachers available for hire, Jameson had thanked God many times for this terrific personnel find.

With good intentions to equip his faculty and staff better for the changing times and changing demographics, Jameson asked two guest presenters to take his faculty through an intensive, one-day workshop on diversity training and culturally responsive teaching, to be enhanced with three half-day training sessions throughout the school year (fall, winter, spring). The two guests who were presenting today, Eugene Patterson and Margaret Slinger, came highly recommended by the local superintendent of the public school system. Apparently, Patterson and Slinger had helped their faculty, staff, and school board train and work through diversity issues during their fall break.

The morning session, however, did not start out as Jameson anticipated or hoped. While Mr. Patterson, a middle-aged African American gentleman, worked hard to listen and get to know the mostly white staff through a quick series of mixers, Ms. Slinger, a younger white woman, came right out of the gate with some shock-and-awe tactics. While introducing herself, she claimed to be bisexual even though her identity was "fluid" depending on the season. Immanuel, "this church school" according to Slinger, was to be commended for evolving and growing with the times. She appreciated the invitation to speak. "Love is love, is love, is love, is love, is love, right? Love always wins! Right?"

Slinger then asked each faculty member to write down their unintended and covert biases and the blind spots they may have due to their white privilege. Her insinuations and assumptions irked several faculty members and put them on the defensive from the start. Most disturbing, she actually made comments that "everyone should speak his or her own truth" and that "anyone who claimed to know the truth is arrogant." *Wasn't she speaking her own truth by making that statement?* many faculty members wondered silently, well-informed of postmodern dogmas. When Slinger put them in small groups to discuss and answer her questions, Jameson felt the icy stares of his faculty and staff. They obviously were questioning his judgment in selecting Slinger to lead these workshops. Jameson was already regretting his decision too.

After Slinger had the faculty members take a bias self-reflection test obviously informed with an LGBTQ agenda, Jameson noticed his own self-reflection test score categorized him as biased against LGBTQ members. Other members of the staff scored the same. Dumbfounded, nervous, and a bit defensive, many of the faculty shut down and refused to participate or say much when called upon to comment on their findings. Slinger picked on Marianna to talk. She wanted to know if Immanuel's "only teacher of color" felt any sort of discrimination and wondered if her voice and input were heard and considered. Did she have a safe spot or place to go when treated inequitably? When Marianna warmly articulated her love for Immanuel and described how the faculty and staff were all brothers and sisters in Christ, that they were one body with many parts, Slinger looked at her incredulously. Religious fanaticism and institutional Christianity, she reminded the entire group, remain two of the most oppressive forces in the world today. She should be on guard, Slinger warned Marianna, for any slippery slope or sign of hidden microaggressions, triggers, or discrimination.

Like many others, Jameson had heard enough from Slinger. Right before he was about to stand up and defend his faculty, Patterson and Slinger declared it was time for a lunch break. After the faculty and staff escaped the room, Jameson confronted Patterson and Slinger, telling both that they had come on a little strong and made allegations or judgments of his personnel that they knew nothing about. Slinger demurred and insisted she was only trying to get them to see their own biases and prejudices. "What I asked you to do," Jameson told both of them, "is to help us be more aware and culturally sensitive to those students who may not look exactly like us or have the same backgrounds as us. I want us to learn better ways to listen and connect with students of color or who have different backgrounds." Both Slinger and Patterson stared at Jameson as he continued. "I want us to become a more united faculty as we prepare to serve a more diverse group of students, but I'm afraid you only played to their worst fears. I want more unity and less divisiveness." He paused. "And Ms. Slinger, I didn't know you were gay or outspoken about your sexual orientation."

"What difference does that make?" she interjected.

"It matters a great deal," Jameson rejoined immediately. "We are a Christian school. We welcome students from all backgrounds and different walks of life here at Immanuel, including those who may feel that they have gay or lesbian tendencies."

"Feel?" Slinger interrupted. "Tendencies?"

"While we welcome all students," Jameson continued, "we do not allow, condone, or lift up sinful behavior or lifestyles."

"That's bigotry and hate speech, Mr. Jameson," Slinger stated defiantly.

"It may be hate speech to you, but for us it's the truth and God's Word," Jameson responded. "Maybe you shouldn't be here for the afternoon session, Ms. Slinger. I apologize. It's my fault that I didn't do my homework better. You will receive your full payment as promised."

Surprised that Patterson chose not to leave with his colleague, Jameson wearily agreed to let Patterson continue with his part of the presentation in the afternoon. Patterson reassured Jameson that "you will like what I have to share with your team, I promise you."

Workshop: Afternoon Session

Surprisingly, almost every faculty and staff member returned for the afternoon session. Eugene Patterson started his presentation by sitting in a chair with the Immanuel faculty and staff surrounding him in a semicircle. He purposely designed the room to create a more intimate setting. "I apologize for this morning," he said. "My colleague can come off a little strong," he explained, trying to walk the fine line of being supportive of Slinger but also offering an olive branch to the host school.

"I truly do appreciate that most of you are white, and yet you want to know more about how you can engage and serve students of color." He continued by sharing a little personal biography: "I went to primarily all-white schools all of my years in education. So I want to say right away: I know most white people are not racist, though some are, and even more than you may think have some prejudices or ideas that they might not realize inhibit students of color from being all they can be and successful in life." He paused for effect. "What I want to share with you, and have some great conversations about, is what I think you can do to help students who are just like I was. And it's all right if you want to challenge some of the things I say. In fact, I think you should. Get your concerns out on the table. I promise I will not judge or disrespect your views. Does that sound okay?" Patterson's earnest introduction contrasted starkly with Slinger's pugnaciousness.

Patterson told many stories of his uncomfortable experiences in school and life in general. He recalled times teachers were quicker to send him to the principal's office when he talked in class or violated the dress code compared to his white peers. When he turned in a well-done assignment, teachers questioned him for plagiarism or accused him of copying other people's work, but they rarely acted the same way toward white students. Since most middle and high schools tracked their students, he was rarely given an opportunity to sign up for more advanced and rigorous classes. "That 'soft bigotry of low expectations' statement that President George W. Bush made famous was true for me," he concurred.

He also explained how white people need to understand that a lot of black people do, in fact, look at everything through the lens of race, whether they should or not. He explained that storekeepers followed him around when he was a teenager—wherever he shopped—and still often did today. Then he asked some question for the group to ponder: why is chocolate cake referred to as *devil's food cake*, while white cake is called *angel food cake*? Why is a troublemaker child referred to as the *black* sheep of the family? Why are deep, *dark* secrets *bad* secrets? Patterson went on to explain that Jesus, whom he loved, is often depicted as white in paintings and pictures and not as a darker-skinned Middle Eastern man. Why? Many blacks did not understand why so many white people so strongly defended the Confederate flag or the slaveholding founding fathers. He could go on with other complaints and concerns (police brutality, incarceration, the criminal justice system, and many other hot-button cultural issues), but he wanted to share what students of color really needed, especially in schools with a more white-majority population: empathy, compassion, trust, fairness, teachers who would not judge but who would approach each student with a glass-half-full attitude instead of a half-empty one, teachers who were looking to catch kids doing something right rather than something wrong. Understand, too, he said, that many students of color want a relationship with their teachers, but only if the relationship is real and genuine, not canned or designed by some textbook. Patterson stopped talking because he noticed a few hands up from the faculty. "Go ahead and have at it," he encouraged. "What do you want to know?"

Immanuel faculty members finally felt comfortable enough with the presenter that they did not hold back in commenting on Patterson's assertions or in asking questions. One by one, they participated in the discussion. Did he understand that white people, students included, often got tired of being accused of using code words or dog-whistle politics for racist purposes when they were simply promoting law and order, hard work, and the American Dream? Didn't black people understand how insulting or frustrating it was to be labeled or called a racist simply for being conservative or belonging to a certain political party? Other teachers insisted that if black people would "throw the 'good' white people a bone" once in a while by acknowledging that most white people were not racist, as Patterson had stated at the beginning of his afternoon presentation, that gesture would go far in the fight for social justice. Other teachers asked for more specific ways they could close the achievement gap—what kinds of scaffolding and best practices worked well for students of color? Even as Patterson and the faculty and staff members disagreed among themselves on certain issues, the conversation continued to ascend in richness. Jameson was pleased.

Finally, the director of Christian education, Craig McClellan, who taught the seventh- and eighth-grade religion classes at Immanuel, stood to make a comment. He had carefully observed the conversations all afternoon and had not said anything until now. "Mr. Patterson," he started. "I want to thank you for your candor and for spending time with us this afternoon. We all need to learn and grow in this area. I know I certainly do." He continued: "My question for you, and for all of us here, is that Scripture is very clear that God loves diversity *and* unity. He only made one of each of us, He knows the number of hairs on each of our heads, Jesus died for all people and each one of us, and God commands each of us to witness about His mercy and grace to all people and all nations." Mr. Patterson nodded at McClellan's comments. "But too often, I feel, our current age highlights and focuses on division, identity politics, celebrating uniqueness, individualism, finding your own truth—my point is that we hear a lot about diversity right now, so much so that it overshadows any thoughts or comments about unity. We don't hear the secular world talking about how we—all people—are one blood, as the Scriptures say, and that we are all children of the same heavenly Father, that we are both saint and sinner alike. Do you think that all this emphasis on diversity, necessary as it may be, has hurt our sense of unity? I'd like to know what you think about that, but also, more important for those of us called to serve God and not humankind here at Immanuel Lutheran School, what does this mean in regard to your teaching and relationships with students and families?"

Reflection and Discussion

The Bible is full of passages in regard to diversity and unity. As you take time to read some of the verses below, reflect on how God's Word on diversity and unity might inform your teaching and leading, and what it means for you as a minister of the Gospel. Since there are so many passages here, consider dividing the texts among pairs in your group and sharing them with one another that way: Revelation 7:9–10; James 2:1–13; 1 Corinthians 12:15–19; Malachi 2:10; 1 Corinthians 14:26; Revelation 14:6; Matthew 28:19–20; Galatians 3:28; Colossians 3:11; 1 Corinthians 1:10; Romans 2:11; Acts 1:8; Isaiah 56:7; Luke 13:29; Ephesians 4:1–7; Titus 3:10–11; Romans 1:16; Proverbs 22:2; Mark 13:10.

1. How would you have reacted to the morning session if you had been there? What would you have said or done as the principal or as a teacher in regard to Margaret Slinger's presentation or approach?
2. What did you like or dislike about Eugene Patterson's presentation?
3. What did you think of some of the teachers' comments or questions directed at Patterson?

BEAR ONE ANOTHER'S BURDENS

The Insidious Impact of Childhood Trauma

BY MICHAEL UDEN

Surveying the list of questions, Mr. Jude grew increasingly agitated. In his eighteen years of teaching, screening protocols for attention-deficit/hyperactivity disorder (ADHD) were tests he tired of seeing his students pass so regularly.

Andrew Jude, fourth-grade teacher at Rocky Mountain Christian Preparatory School in Sun Peak, Colorado, often bristled at standardized tests of any variety. His perspective was that a solitary score, while able to provide some information, was a single variable within a much more complex algorithm: the life of a human being. His pedagogy underscored that belief, as he established authentic relationships with his students as well as their families and cultivated those relationships throughout strong seasons of development. Growing up on a farm, Andy learned early that if a plant is not growing well, one studies and adjusts the plant's environment (sunlight, water, soil, fertilizer) rather than simply uprooting the seedling to another farm or, worse yet, to the compost pile.

Today, he was considering all he knew about Marissa Schumacher, a new student to Rocky Mountain Christian Prep, who had joined his fourth grade shortly after this school year had begun. Marissa was a quiet girl, although that was not unusual for a nine-year-old suddenly in a new place without the security of classmates she had known since kindergarten. Marissa and her mother relocated to the area to move in with her stepfather, as he and Marissa's mother had married late last summer. Marissa was the only child in the household, and she appeared to be in a loving and supportive home. For example, Mr. Jude was pleased to see both her mother and stepfather at parent-teacher conferences, and he spied Marissa's stepfather at the school's fall fine arts festival by himself when her mother was traveling for business. For Andy Jude, investing in others was second nature; however, he also recognized that when families blend, establishing the balance of "yours, mine, and ours," especially with children, could be a delicate process for all involved.

Marissa had not shared much about her life prior to Rocky Mountain and Sun Peak. As was his practice, Mr. Jude devoted his Tuesday and Thursday lunch periods to one-on-one dining with his students. Progressing through his class, he had lunched with Marissa twice so far this year. In their first conversation, he learned Marissa's parents had divorced before her birth and that her biological father had never been part of her life. Marissa's mom, a sales representative for a large technology company, met her new stepdad at a trade show. As their courtship progressed to engagement, the couple decided to live in his home within the picturesque Sun Peak community. This prompted a move for Marissa from Denver, where she had lived her entire life. The distance between the two locations was relatively small (thirty miles), so Marissa could visit and stay connected with friends, but Andy recognized that her former life in Denver and all that she had known seemed at times to be on the other side of the world.

During their second lunch, Marissa talked exclusively—and often glowingly—about her best friend, Hannah. Andy was amused, both by the shift in Marissa's countenance as she recounted her lifelong friendship, as well as her classmates' reactions, seated just a few feet from their table. Marissa was typically distant in class, so they seemed surprised—and excited—to witness this new dimension of her personality. When her eyes teared up toward the end of the conversation, Mr. Jude believed he realized how close the two friends were and how greatly Marissa apparently missed Hannah.

The winsome recollection of these conversations was hijacked by the protocol he still needed to complete. Does the student demonstrate distractibility? Irritability? Does the student seem unable to follow a sequence of directions? Ironically, Marissa's score on this screening might be higher than any test she had taken while at Rocky Mountain Prep, Andy winced to himself. More uncomfortable to him was the realization of what his completed protocol might prompt. Too often, well-meaning pediatricians and often-desperate parents rushed toward pharmaceutical solutions. Medication was warranted in some cases, but he felt less convinced that it was the best or only solution in others. Frankly, he was not confident the issue was always ADHD. Growing up, he recalled how his classroom attention more than waned when spring sunshine made its first appearance or when his mind was occupied elsewhere. He considered how he might have fared had his teachers been asked to complete a similar protocol on him.

Saint Jude, as he was affectionately nicknamed by more than a few of his classroom parents, had a reputation as a kid whisperer. Rocky Mountain Christian Preparatory was not a Catholic academy, although Mr. Jude often appeared to be a patron saint of lost children. He embodied both the art and science of teaching, due to authentic relationships as well as his common-sense approach to the nine- and ten-year-old species. As an example, it was not uncommon for him to host literature circles in the clover of the school's back fields. He fought hardest among the faculty to maintain the school's generous noon recess when a new Rocky Mountain Prep administrator was determined to find more instructional minutes in the school day. He won that battle due to his dogged determination on behalf of the kids as well as his data. Andy Jude remembered the growing pains—physical and emotional—of childhood.

Years earlier, he had connected with Corrine Chapman, then a young social work intern serving at the Department for Veterans Affairs, where Andy's uncle received ongoing services. Uncle Bill was not killed during his service in Vietnam, but, as Andy's family would recount, his service in Vietnam was what ultimately killed him. Even before his Vietnam homecoming, Bill Jude was wracked by addiction. While he neither married nor had children, Bill was faithfully served by his nephew Andy.

After her internship at the VA, Corrine began her career as a school social worker; she and Andy, who initially connected during Bill's regular appointments, stayed in touch as friends. When the great recess war of 2010 hit his school, Andy emailed his friend Corrine, who armed him with mounds of data regarding the value of physical activity on cognition, particularly in children, as well as the specific benefits of recess for children who struggled with reading or mathematics.

The consultative connection between Corrine and Andy was not limited to recess duty. She had served as Andy's guide when he faced a tough call as a mandated reporter, and he had aided her when she needed a broader perspective on whether a choking game she learned about from a child in her school was a larger phenomenon. This symbiotic relationship and their shared interest in the best interests of children enriched the work of them both as well as the hundreds of children they both served.

A few weeks after Marissa's completed protocol had been submitted, Mr. and Mrs. Hendrich, Marissa's stepfather and mother, asked to meet with Mr. Jude in order to discuss the action plan. Marissa had been prescribed Adderall, and Andy's feedback on its effects on her during the day would be integral, especially as the dosage was regulated. Certainly, Andy viewed himself as a partner in this process, but he found himself in the role of counselor during his meeting with Marissa's family. Mr. Hendrich attempted to reassure himself, as he kept restating, "I know this is for the best. We have to do something." This decision had been challenging for all of them, and Andy had nearly accepted this course until he heard Mrs. Hendrich add, "I just don't know how this could have developed now."

"What you mean by that?" Andy pursued. The cumulative records from Marissa's last school had not yet made their way to her new school. Mr. Jude reeled at the realization he may have assumed far too much about Marissa's academic history.

"Marissa has always been a solid student and focused on her work," Marissa's mother continued, "but things are so different for her here. You have been so kind to her—and us—Mr. Jude, but the curriculum is obviously more rigorous. The doctor even told us that conditions like the ones we are seeing in Marissa are not always evident until after the primary grades. So, it all makes sense, right?" Mrs. Hendrich seemed eager to reassure herself.

Andy attempted to remain fully present in the conversation and empathetic to those across from him at the table. Still, his mind was racing as he considered again the other causes for Marissa's recent struggles.

"Certainly, there are times when gaps in cognitive processing can become more apparent," he began, "but it is also possible that ADHD may not be accurate for Marissa. As her teacher and your ally, I urge you to pause this process and look at all possible factors."

"Such as?" Mr. Hendrich interjected.

"I do not know," Saint Jude acknowledged, "but I would like to consult with some colleagues who may."

Moments later, Andy emailed Corrine to see if she could talk by phone that evening. Yet relief at her open schedule quickly was quelled by fear of the unknown. What might Marissa be facing to cause such a shift in her academic performance? Fortunately, Corrine's vast experience provided her vantage points Andy did not have.

"So, you are telling me that she is highly distractible in class and often seems to struggle in remembering even the broadest components of a class activity?" Corrine questioned. "Help me understand more about her life outside of school. Any changes there?"

Andy described what he knew of Marissa's life during the past year: a move to Sun Peak, her mom's second marriage, a new school, adjustment to life with a stepfather, and so on. Corrine listened intently, affirmed Andy for his comprehensive approach to helping the family, and then provided an idea regarding a diagnosis.

"What many people, even educators, don't realize," Corrine began, "are parallels between how ADHD and trauma present themselves in the classroom. The symptoms seen are nearly identical. This is the 'what.' Yet the 'why' behind such classroom performance and behavior is a much different story."

"Trauma?" Andy was reeling at this realization. "Marissa has been through a lot in the past year, but is it traumatic? Her stepfather has been phenomenal throughout this whole process. I read people, Corrine, and I see no indication that he or her mother are anything but absolutely in Marissa's corner."

Corrine valued Andy's zeal, but she needed him to understand more. "Andy," she coaxed, "there is no standardized scoring for how children process life events and experiences. Even children from the same family are affected differently by the same event, be it the divorce of parents or even a death. Individual factors, such as resiliency, can vary greatly."

Andy nodded, recalling how differently he and his sister had processed Uncle Bill's death. "I get it, but I cannot account for the shift Marissa has made academically. When her mother describes her academic ability and performance from previous years, we see nothing in common with where she is now."

"Another insight for those seeking to support children potentially affected by trauma is not to assume we understand the cause," Corrine continued. "Things are not always as they seem. I recently worked with a young woman whose mother had just passed away after months in hospice."

"Oh, man," Andy empathized.

"Of course, that's a significant loss," Corrine responded, "but grief and mourning are natural processes whose most direct impacts lessen over time."

"So, if it continues too long, it's trauma?" Andy guessed.

"When children continue to experience profound struggles, something needs to be understood better. Again, we practitioners must remember not to assume. In the case of the girl I referenced, while she missed her mom dearly, that was not the reason for the struggles she was experiencing months later."

"What was?" Andy asked fearfully.

"After talking with and learning from her what she had experienced, I learned it was about a dog."

"Excuse me?" Andy was both relieved and confused.

"Well," Corrine explained, "she had her own dog, which she had loved for years. When she visited her mom in hospice, there was a comfort dog on site with which she had many special conversations as well. Dogs sustained her. Once her mom died, her dad—trying to do the best he could for his daughter—arranged for her to stay with a neighbor lady after school until he could be home from work."

"That was good, right?" Andy hesitated.

"It seemed to be the best care possible," Corrine reassured him.

"The neighbor was delightful and doting, but also dog-free. Without canine companions to help her decompress after school, my young friend became anxious. Her stress translated to sleeplessness, and her days were preoccupied with fears that something might happen to her beloved pet."

"It was about a dog," Andy summarized incredulously.

Corrine confirmed, "The cause and the experience for one who has endured trauma can vary widely. Sometimes children experience trauma directly. Other times they are affected by a trauma that may have happened to someone else, even a stranger. Remember 9/11?" Corrine inquired.

"Absolutely. It was my second year of teaching, and I had no idea what to do. My class just watched the planes crashing into the towers over and over that day," Andy recounted.

"Children nationwide did the same thing, in the care of educators who were too numb to proceed differently. In the months following, however, we saw the vicarious impact of trauma. Very few of the students watching the footage knew anyone in the World Trade Center or in close proximity to ground zero, but thousands of children were traumatized by what they experienced secondhand," Corrine explained.

"Unbelievable." Andy's mind was full, as he drew the connection between the horror witnessed by children on 9/11 with the horrors his Uncle Bill had seen in Vietnam decades before.

"Our job is to listen, learn, and then help young people see themselves as survivors rather than victims."

Mr. Jude was a careful student in that conversation, and he both listened and learned a great deal from Corrine. First, he connected Marissa's family with a local counselor who specialized in trauma, and Marissa was eventually able to identify the source of her anxiety. Hannah, her best friend, after swearing Marissa to secrecy months earlier, had recounted the sexual assault she was experiencing at the hands of her mom's live-in boyfriend.

Marissa was not only overwhelmed by fear and concern for Hannah, but she was also overcome by parallels to her own life. She and her mom had moved into a house with a new man as well. While absolutely no abuse had occurred by her stepfather, Marissa was processing trauma she was experiencing vividly, albeit vicariously, from her dearest friend. The transition to a new school, coupled with a business travel season for her mother, placed Marissa in the eye of the perfect storm.

"I would have done anything to reassure Marissa," Mr. Hendrich relayed in Mr. Jude's classroom during the spring parent-teacher conferences, his eyes welling with tears. "Thank you so much for encouraging us to look further," he continued, shaking Andy's hand.

"Christ calls us to bear one another's burdens," Andy responded. "We strive to do that here at Rocky Mountain Christian Prep, but Marissa was also attempting to do just that for Hannah." And what Uncle Bill did for years following Vietnam, Andy thought to himself. "I am looking at a lot of things with new eyes," Mr. Jude concluded.

Reflection and Discussion

The burden of trauma falls on many more than just the individual person injured. As part of the Body of Christ, when one member hurts, the whole Body hurts. Read and discuss the following passages and their various applications for this chapter: 1 Peter 5:7; Psalm 107:13–16; Matthew 11:28–30.

1. The effects of trauma can be very individualized, meaning that two children who experienced the same event may be affected very differently. What implications does this have for a classroom teacher?
2. It is vital for educators to consider the "what" of a situation (that is, the student behaviors being evidenced) but not to stop there. We must always attempt to determine the "why" as well. Why are both elements important?
3. Where do you feel Mr. Jude, the classroom teacher, responded admirably to the situation? In what areas would you have recommended a different course of action for him?
4. Trauma notwithstanding, assimilating into a new school environment can be tough for a student. What do you do to ease that transition for all involved?

A TALE OF A TROUBLEMAKER TURNED CREATOR

BY BERNARD BULL

You couldn't find a more curious and committed student than Janet. She had an incredible thirst for knowledge. She wasn't a documented genius—far from that. Janet worked hard to understand new ideas. It sometimes took her twice as long to read a book, but she seemed to enjoy it twice as much as anybody else. It was just that she loved learning.

At the same time, Janet was not a big fan of school policies and practices. Because she was so curious, she liked to question just about any policy or practice in school. It wasn't that she was trying to be a troublemaker, although she did enjoy a good debate. In fact, she seemed to learn a great deal through debates, so she looked forward to them. In addition, she didn't always give school leaders or teachers the benefit of the doubt. She had this craving to understand why, and she enjoyed being a part of making decisions that impacted her education. When her input wasn't welcome, she could get a little frustrated. She wasn't violent or verbally abusive, but she clearly didn't like it very much. She wanted to learn, and while it didn't all need to be on her terms, she certainly thrived when a teacher gave her voice and input on the learning experience.

This independent streak is what most teachers noticed. Plenty of teachers tired of Janet's curiosity and questions. They interpreted it as disrespectful and thought that it detracted from a positive classroom environment. Some dealt with her questions through formal disciplinary action, so Janet was not unfamiliar with after-school detention. Others just did their best to ignore her, pretending like they didn't see her hand raised when Janet had something to say. Janet wasn't oblivious to this strategy. She would eventually just check out, so perhaps the teachers saw it as an effective strategy.

Janet didn't give up on people or school, no matter how much people seemed to struggle with her personality. Each day, she came to school ready to learn something new. She didn't always come to school the most prepared, but she was definitely excited to learn something new, to experience something new, to have great conversations about ideas that mattered to her and the world. So, she stayed positive and looked for classes, teachers, and opportunities to explore and learn. Some days were better than others, but she had incredible persistence.

One day, Janet overheard some of the teachers talking about a new experiment at the school. The principal challenged a few creative teachers to help research and explore the possibility of creating a school-within-a-school, an experimental project-based-learning program. Students would have the opportunity to apply to be part of the new program. As she listened to them talk about this over lunch, she couldn't help herself. Janet was not short on confidence, so she walked over to the teachers, one of whom was her social studies teacher, and mentioned that she overheard what they were talking about. She asked if there might be any possibility for her to help as a student advisor on this project, to give a student perspective.

She realized that asking this was a long shot, but she was delighted when they both responded in the affirmative. In fact, they had not thought of getting a student view, and they charged her to find two more classmates who would be willing to serve on a student advisory board for this project. She gladly accepted that challenge, and she and two student volunteers were ready for an after-school meeting the very next day.

During that after-school meeting, the lead teachers on the project introduced the challenge, the goal, and the timeline. They had six months to put together a full plan for a special project-based-learning school-within-a-school. This included researching promising examples from other schools, creating a detailed plan of what it would look like and how it would work, and doing research to find out how many students would be interested in such a program. They even had to build a budget. While the teachers were the leaders of the project, they indicated that they wanted the students to be involved with each of these parts, as long as the project didn't interfere with their regular schoolwork.

Over the next months, Janet, these two teachers, and the other two students met several times a week. They planned. They researched. They reached out to other project-based-learning schools, interviewing teachers and students about what worked and what did not work. They learned about the costs of such a school. They read articles and discussed them. They also worked together to create a thirty-page proposal that outlined the plans for this new school. This was one of the most exhilarating learning experiences of Janet's formal schooling experience.

In a culminating moment, the teachers and students had the opportunity to present their plan to the principal and some representatives from the school board. The two teachers did most of the presenting, but they gave each of the students three to five minutes to share their insights and contributions to the work. The students were particularly inspired by visiting and learning about examples of other project-based schools and classrooms.

When it was Janet's turn to speak, she began by explaining that she was a very curious person. She liked to ask lots of questions. She liked to debate and explore ideas. She was self-aware enough to know that this didn't always go over well in some of her classes. While she didn't mean to do so, she acknowledged that she could be disruptive. Yet when she visited and learned about some of these project-based schools, she found many students just like her. They asked lots of questions. They discussed and debated. They also learned how to develop that curiosity and become more focused and disciplined. Of course, some students struggled with procrastination or a lack of organization, but these schools seemed to have ways to help students work through these challenges. Janet finished her talk with this statement: "I love being at this school. Going to a Christian school is important to me. I also love asking questions and exploring. If we could put the two of those together, I feel like it would be perfect for me, and plenty of other students like me."

The principal and board members were impressed with the overall presentation. The teachers leading the projects did great work compiling a plan for the new school, including a financial plan that was achievable. A few weeks later, the entire group was delighted to find out that a couple board members donated a small amount of money to help fund a pilot and experimental year of the program. Also, when the project was approved and announced to launch the next year, guess who was the first person to register?

Reflection and Discussion

1. Was Janet a troublemaker? Explain.
2. Can you think of students such as Janet in your school? How are they perceived by others?
3. In some ways, this case represents a rather rare opportunity, perhaps a scenario less likely to occur at many schools. However, are there any lessons or ideas that emerge about how you could engage some of the "troublemakers" in your school in a similar way?
4. In this story, students are engaged in helping to create or design something new in the school. What role do students currently play in helping to design and create at your school? What possible ways could you engage them in this sort of work?

FOSTERING ACCEPTANCE AND UNDERSTANDING

A Foster Child in Another New School

BY MICHAEL UDEN

"Christ the Life Academy, Christ the Life Academy," Tyler Watson repeated to himself over and over as he stepped off the school bus. He had found that having simple information at the ready, such as current address, birthday, or school you attend, helped in small talk with people you might encounter. People did not know him and would not get to know him, he realized, but at least he would stand out less.

When Tyler had been delivered to the home of Lucas and Amy Kleinfeldt three months earlier, he had quizzed himself on the new address in much the same way. This home was different than the last place he had lived, but if there was one thing that Tyler Watson had learned in his fourteen years of life, it was that things never stay as they start. He would be ready for the next disappointment, the next move, the next home address and school name to memorize, whenever the need became apparent.

For now, though, he was establishing a rudimentary routine. Mrs. Kleinfeldt, who invited Tyler to call her Amy, was different than his last foster mom. She would look at him directly when she spoke to him in a way he had not experienced, perhaps ever. Her voice was gentle and inviting, like one used to coax a skittish cat down from a dangerous limb of a tree. For his part, Tyler had been tiptoeing around danger long before he moved to the Kleinfeldts.

His mom always looked at him straight in the eyes, Tyler recollected, but the cast of her eyes and the timbre of her voice were not always consistent. Sometimes she was gentle and soft, like a princess heroine. Tyler embraced the memory of that tone before it evaporated from his consciousness. It was becoming harder to call up that one, but he must not lose it from his memory. Tyler chided himself for not being more careful, wincing as he realized again how he was no longer able to remember the laugh of his father—or at least the man who had filled that role during the first four years of Tyler Watson's life.

Other memories of his mom's communication were not a fairy tale. While she would still stare at him directly, her voice could be more frantic or faltering. Her eyes revealed fear or loathing, although Tyler was never certain as to why or for whom. Most days, he stopped thinking about any of the *why* factors. It was too exhausting to solve an equation in which so many variables were missing.

Lucas and Amy Kleinfeldt appeared safe so far. Their house seemed as big as an entire floor of the apartment building where he and his mom had last lived, and they let Tyler go anywhere in the house. Tyler had learned that this was not the case in every foster home. In the last house, he had a bedroom on the first floor off the living room, but he was not allowed to go upstairs where the "real family" slept. In his first foster house, he lived with two women who had no lock on the bathroom door. Tyler learned to wait to do his business at school or at a store because he did not like how they always walked in on him.

The young Mr. Watson took a deep breath as he approached the door of his latest classroom. Mr. Hasselmeyer, the teacher, always greeted Tyler as he entered, although sometimes it caught Tyler off-guard. He could not remember a time in his life when men such as Lucas and Mr. Hasselmeyer stayed nice for so long. His mom had been with a number of men since his alleged dad had stepped out of their picture—enough that Tyler had a baby brother, Tony—but kindness always had a motive. One past boyfriend would give Tyler money to leave the apartment for the day with his little brother. Another man who had seemed nice came into the bathroom while Tyler was in the shower. Tyler heard him taking off clothes and felt confused as to what was happening. He tried to make himself small so he could be invisible to anyone around him. Sometimes at the new school, he tried to do the same. People always saw him and found him, though.

Mr. Hasselmeyer had been a teacher for a long time, Tyler recalled. If he had figured the math correctly using the date from the college diploma that hung on the classroom wall—and Tyler was certain he had, because it was one of his rituals each day—Brent Hasselmeyer had been teaching for thirty years. Mom had turned thirty years old before Tyler had left, and she had never looked as vibrant as his teacher. Of course, Mr. Hasselmeyer spent a lot of time talking about Jesus Christ, and that man seemed to be older than anyone else.

Tyler had been trying to piece together who Jesus Christ truly was at this new school, Christ the Life. It appeared the school was named for him, like a McDonald's. Jesus had a number of business ventures, because Tyler saw Mr. Hasselmeyer on the weekends too. He attended the church where his foster family went every week. In fact, Mr. Hasselmeyer taught another school just on Sunday morning, and Tyler was in that class as well. The other kids in both of Tyler's classes seemed to understand everything there was to know about Jesus Christ. Not only could they answer questions, but they could also recite parts of other books that He had written or were written about Him. For his part, Tyler tried to keep Jesus' biography straight, but there were so many other things he was already trying to remember—like his birthday and his address—that he spent most of the time just sitting still in class and hoping not to be noticed or called on. He again tried desperately to be small, even invisible. Mr. Hasselmeyer never yelled or embarrassed him or made him feel like he should know more. Tyler felt relief in that temporary calm as he frequently walked through storms.

As an example, one day, Tyler overheard some kids talking about his latest foster family. Apparently Lucas and Amy had met with the mother of one of his classmates. She was the president of some board that gave money to pay for Christ the Life Academy. It seemed the Kleinfeldts had plenty of money, but the classmate relaying the story indicated it involved financial aid for "a ward of the state." Tyler knew his mother had given permission for him to go to Christ the Life when the Kleinfeldts requested it, but he had not realized it cost money. In Tyler's estimation, Mr. Hasselmeyer was the best teacher he had ever had and certainly deserved a lot of pay, but Tyler was now self-conscious for the trouble he had caused. He was also struck by the irony that his classmates spoke far more words when talking about him than they ever did in talking to him.

It was not a surprise to Tyler that his mom had given her permission for him to attend Christ the Life Academy, although he did acknowledge his surprise that the Kleinfeldts had been able to locate her long enough to obtain the signature. Mom yelled out to "Jesus Christ" throughout Tyler's childhood, although her tone was different than when Mr. Hasselmeyer spoke to Him. Tyler even recalled his mother screaming along to "Jesus Take the Wheel" on the radio before actually letting go of her steering wheel while in traffic. The police officers at the station gave Tyler as much hot chocolate as he wanted that night, so he held a fond first glimpse of what this Jesus guy was capable of doing.

At this point in his life, Tyler's favorite times were spent alone. He could do what he chose, he could feel what he wanted, and he would never frighten or leave himself. Other people hurt you in the end or left before you had a chance to say goodbye. Tyler trained himself never to get too close to anyone. Each day, he focused on getting through and fitting in as best he could. Life as a foster child made that more challenging, though, because so much still depended on his mother, who had long before established she was not a reliable source.

Every two weeks, Tyler was supposed to visit his mom. The transport company would pull up in an ugly green van and drive him to an ugly building where Tyler and his mother were supposed to spend two hours together. When he was in the first foster home, Tyler remembered feeling so excited at the chance to see his mom. He thought about which of his jeans were cleanest for the visit, and he imagined the reunion they would enjoy.

Tyler's imagination sometimes filled in where his life failed to produce. He sat in his good jeans for two hours at the ugly building before the ugly van took him back to the two women and the bathroom door that did not lock. At least he had been able to use the restroom while waiting for his mother. There were other visits when his mom did show, but Tyler really wanted to go back to his home to spend time with her there. Mom would explain she was moving or her place was a mess or the ugly building was closer for Tyler. More words, more excuses, more time wasted. Tyler learned to expect disappointment so he would not be surprised by the hurt.

Even when his mom came less and less frequently, Tyler looked forward to the two-hour visits. In his mind, he would imagine that he was a celebrity being chauffeured by a driver in his employ. When his mother was a no-show, sometimes his guardian *ad litem* (GAL), Lucille Montcrief, would visit and let him pick out a treat from the ugly building's vending machine. When Tyler lived at the home where he could not go upstairs, he even got to see his brother Tony a few times. Later that summer, he learned Tony was to be adopted by another family. They were planning to change Tony's name, and Tyler could not remember the new name or even very much about how Tony looked. He could remember the sound of Tony's cry, but Tyler was disappointed in himself for only having that as a memory so he tried not to think about his brother at all. Tyler's weekend visits now gave him what he liked best: time by himself with no one to rely upon but Tyler.

Tyler recognized that he did not have friends. Part of that was likely his fault, because he did not ever let people get too close, and part of that blame was squarely on the shoulders of his classmates. Mr. Hasselmeyer did not allow anyone to tease or hurt a classmate, which was different than other schools Tyler had attended. Yet there were some questions that a classmate could ask in conversation that did not appear malicious enough to warrant Mr. Hasselmeyer's attention, even when the student had plotted the intended outcome. Early on, it seemed his Christ the Life Academy classmates were genuinely curious about Tyler as the new student. Initially, they chided him about his unkempt hair.

Tyler had not grown up visiting a barber, although he passed three of them on his Saturday drives to the visits in the ugly building. Lucas and Amy Kleinfeldt had reassured him that he could get a haircut whenever and however he wanted, so they were surprised to learn that haircuts required permission from Tyler's mom, as did much of his life in foster care. For that reason, when one of Tyler's classmates obligatorily invited him to a birthday sleepover at the start of the year, the Kleinfeldts had to explain that as much as they would love for Tyler to attend, his mom was still the only one to provide that consent. Tyler would always love his mom, despite all of her faults, but he had long ago determined she was not the most reliable adult. At age 6, Tyler would scrounge for change in the apartment and hide it so they would have money to buy milk at the end of the month.

Tyler realized that the woman who left her kids with a man she had only met two days before was likely not a viable candidate to sign off on a sleepover. While the Kleinfeldts had done all they could to advocate for Tyler, GAL Montcrief had indicated the state was working to file termination in his case. They did not want to seek temporary guardianship prematurely, or it might give his mom's appointed defender grounds for a stronger appeal. Tyler was numbed by more words and more waiting, as he recognized that for now—and perhaps for his entire life—he would be the guy with the weird hair who was never again invited to a sleepover. Knowing his fate at least meant there would not be surprises. Surprises often hurt, and Tyler always wanted to be aware and in control. That was better.

The Kleinfeldts' only biological child, sixth-grade Arianna, was the closest thing to a friend Tyler had. She smiled a lot like Amy, her mother, but her laugh was completely her own. Loud as a freight train, it would emerge unannounced at the slightest provocation. At first, this truly alarmed Tyler, who was not accustomed to frivolity. Over time, however, he not only anticipated Arianna's frequent laugh but also schemed ways to entice it. Arianna especially liked when Tyler would impersonate the Christ the Life Academy faculty or even the Kleinfeldts themselves. Always hypervigilant, Tyler memorized the mannerisms and expressions of all who surrounded him, so mimicking was an easy parlor game. Although he did not actually share his inner self with her—Tyler simply impersonated the cast of characters they had in common—it felt good to interact with someone else, even to this degree. Tyler tried hard to capture the sound of Arianna's laugh and save it for a future when he would no longer be able to hear it. It could be a needed balm for Tyler's soul during a terrible tomorrow.

Tyler had become accustomed to the easy rhythm in this latest stop of his life. He liked feeling relatively safe most of the time and interacting with adults from whom he knew what to anticipate. Walking in the front door of the Kleinfeldts' house after school with Arianna, then, he was surprised to see not only Lucas and Amy but also Mr. Hasselmeyer and Ms. Montcrief. His situation quickly seemed discordant again.

"Tyler," Lucas welcomed. "We are so glad to have you as part of our family, and we want to talk about how we can all help you feel more accepted and understood. Each of us cares about you a great deal, and we are here to help however we can."

Tyler felt his face turn red, and his stomach twisted further. Why are they doing this, he pleaded to himself. What are they planning? When will the ugly van come to drive me away? I wish they would all stop looking at me. I wish simply to be invisible so that they could not see me standing here at all or hurt me again. People in my life do not stay, Tyler resigned himself. Things never stay as they start.

Reflection and Discussion

As Christians, we are certainly called to care for one another, even in difficult circumstances. Read and discuss the following passages and their implications in regards to the topic of this chapter: 1 Peter 3:8; Matthew 9:36; Hebrews 13:3; Luke 10:33–34; 1 John 4:7–8.

1. At the end of the case study, there was nothing truly wrong with the intentions of those gathered to help Tyler, but Tyler's past history and current perception signaled to him that everything was wrong and at risk. This contrast between perception and reality is important for teachers to remember. Students' reactions and behaviors are not always about you. What implications does this have for classroom practice?
2. How and to whom should a teacher reach out for support and resources if they are unsure of how to meet the needs of a new student, perhaps specifically a foster child in the classroom?
3. While Tyler's classroom teacher was welcoming, Tyler had not connected well with his classmates. Should a teacher help students navigate peer connections? Why or why not?
4. Many Christian people dismiss the idea of being a foster parent because they think, "I could not care that much about a person who may not stay in my life." What implications does that have for foster children and the foster care system as a whole?

LOSE SOME AND WINSOME TEACHING

Praying at the Pope's Death

BY JIM PINGEL

First Hour

The pope was officially dead. The head of the Roman Catholic Church had died of a massive heart attack overnight. Even with the ebbing media interest in religion (unless there was a scandal to report or hypocrisy to highlight), the pope's passing dominated the news.

An avid fan of all things history, Christ Community Lutheran School's (CCLS) eighth-grade homeroom and social studies teacher, Ms. Kristin Schwartz, had the news projecting on the screen as her students entered the classroom. Three of her students—Meghan, Elizabeth, and Nicholas—expressed great sadness, for this particular pope had been beloved in their Catholic homes. "I'm really sorry for your loss," Ms. Schwartz told each of them. "He seemed like a really caring man and a wonderful Christian leader." The three Catholic students asked Ms. Schwartz if she would include a petition in her prayers for all those mourning over the loss of the holy pontiff. Of course she would include them in her prayers, she told them. Then she gave each of them a hug.

Second Hour

"Okay, settle down, everyone. Settle down!" As students took their seats for theology class, Pastor William Andrews moved to the front of the room behind his podium, on which Martin Luther's seal was prominently displayed. "Any prayer requests this morning?" he asked.

Meghan, Elizabeth, and Nicholas raised their hands. He called on Meghan, who asked if he would pray for all those around the world grieving the pope's death. "Yeah, I heard the news this morning," Pastor Andrews plainly noted, "but we're a Lutheran school so we don't really pray for the pope or his followers." Stunned by their religion teacher's directness, Meghan, Elizabeth, and Nicholas glanced at one another in astonishment. As Elizabeth began to tear up, one of her classmates interjected, "The pope's not perfect, you know." Said another, "Yeah, only Jesus was perfect. What's the big deal about the pope anyway? On television, it looked like he could barely walk or stand." Anger now flashed across Elizabeth's face, but she said nothing. She had no idea Lutherans felt this away about the Holy See.

"Okay, okay, settle down, people. No, the pope is certainly not perfect," Pastor Andrews concurred. "But that's not the reason we don't pray for him. We don't pay homage or honor him because he claims to be a Vicar of Christ, which he's not." Meghan, Elizabeth, and Nicholas were not even sure what "Vicar of Christ" meant. Pastor Andrews continued, "In fact, Luther called the office of the papacy the antichrist. So we don't honor anyone who is anti-Christ or *the* Antichrist, okay?" Pastor Andrews went on, "Every Lutheran teacher here at CCLS took an oath to abide by the Lutheran Confessions," he explained, "which clearly teaches that the office of the papacy or the pope is the antichrist. So we don't pray for the dead, to the supposed saints, or certainly about the pope." Pastor Andrews quickly moved on: "Any other prayer requests?"

"Pastor, is it true that Catholics pray to Mary?" one student earnestly asked.

"What do Catholics believe, anyway?" said another.

"They pray to saints such as Mother Teresa," said a student sitting directly next to Nicholas.

"That's one thing I don't get about Catholics, Pastor," said a girl who belonged to his church. "Why not just connect directly with God and pray to Jesus? Why do they pray to false gods such as their so-called saints?"

The class cutup interjected, "Hey, I'd pray to St. LeBron if it would help my hoop game." Everyone laughed—everyone except Meghan, Elizabeth, and Nicholas.

"Ladies and gentlemen," Pastor Andrews said, after shushing the students, "I'd really like to take prayer requests first. Catholics believe in the traditions of the Church as established by their pope and Church councils, good works, and a bit of Jesus." He looked around the room. "Isn't that right, Meghan, Nicholas, and where is my other Catholic friend, oh, and Elizabeth? Am I portraying your faith accurately?" Meghan and Nicholas looked down at their desks, while Elizabeth glared at Pastor Andrews. "Well, we will talk more about the difference between Catholics and Lutherans in the future, all right? Last call for prayer requests, and then I want to read you an opening devotion on the difference between being a reverend and a pastor."

Third Hour

For several weeks now, Mrs. Sandra Schlicting had been working with the middle school choir as they prepared for the upcoming Reformation service. The choir would be singing the first two stanzas of two powerful and traditional Lutheran hymns: "Thy Strong Word" and "A Mighty Fortress Is Our God." The choir had been making progress, but not fast and far enough for the high standards of Mrs. Schlicting.

"Mrs. Schlicting," asked one sixth grader named Hannah, "can we also sing some praise songs for the Reformation service?"

"These great hymns *are* praise songs, my dear—they're praising God from whom all blessings flow."

"No, I understand. I like these hymns," Hannah replied, "but there are so many other really cool praise songs we could sing too, especially if, say, around a thousand people are coming to this concert. We could really get the crowd excited and feel the love of Christ just pouring down on them!"

"Hannah, I don't need to feel Christ's love raining or pouring down on me," interrupted Mrs. Schlicting. "I know He loves me. He died on the cross for my sins. And it's not a concert; it's a worship service."

"Could we sing 'In Christ Alone'? Or 'The Heart of Worship,' 'Awesome God,' or 'Great and Mighty Is He'? Or even Michael W. Smith's new song? There are so many cool songs we could sing," another student named Ashley inquired.

"Yeah, we sing those at my church, First Reformed Church, all the time," Hannah explained. "People love singing those songs and worshiping at our church. I know I do."

"No, we've already picked out our worship songs from the hymnal," Mrs. Schlicting insisted. "We aren't going to sing or play music with guitars or get people raising the roof," she mimed pushing her arms and hands upward, "or swaying their arms, or talking about giving their heart to Jesus, or repeating the same verse over and over about a hundred times, all right?" Seeing the surprised look in the eyes of Ashley and Hannah, Mrs. Schlicting realized she had come on a bit too strong. She tried to backpedal a bit: "It's fine if you like to listen to that kind of music in the car or at home, or even at your own church, but we take our worship seriously here at CCLS. Martin Luther started the Reformation, so we're going to sing Lutheran hymns After all, we Lutherans are the ones historically known for being a singing church. So we're going to sing these hymns really well and give God the glory, okay?"

Fourth Hour

"Wow, that's beautiful, Tiki," exclaimed Mrs. Laura Dorn, CCLS's art teacher. Affectionately nicknamed *Tiki* by her peers, Ting Kang had come from Shanghai as a foreign exchange student. Her parents were avowed atheists, but they approved Tiki's enrollment at CCLS because of its outstanding academic reputation. Mrs. Dorn's class had been working on their clay projects for a week now, and Tiki had constructed a moving scene of a young girl washing the feet of a woman.

On the first day of every new unit, Mrs. Dorn shared a biblical account or lesson with her students, which they would be required to incorporate into their next project. For this particular week, Mrs. Dorn had selected the story of Jesus washing the feet of His disciples at the Last Supper.

Tiki had barely heard of Jesus before she came to CCLS. In addition to her parents being atheists, Tiki knew many Chinese families who had been arrested for studying the "American holy book" or covertly participating in church services in a basement. Nevertheless, as the weeks passed at CCLS, Tiki heard God's Word in class and during chapel, and the Holy Spirit worked on Tiki's heart and brought her to faith in Christ.

"Now tell me," asked Mrs. Dorn, "why did you decide to go with a woman in this sculpture instead of Jesus?"

"Well, I love Jesus because He saved me from my sins," Tiki explained. "I will show Jesus in my next project. But for this project, I wanted to honor the person who helped me meet Jesus."

"Ah, that's sweet, Tiki," said Mrs. Dorn, oblivious to what was coming next. "So who is this beautiful woman?" she asked, pointing to Tiki's project.

"You, Mrs. Dorn," Tiki asserted. "You teach me about Jesus. You read to me about Him. You are just like Jesus because you served and saved me too." Mrs. Dorn could not muster any words. Stunned and truly touched, she quickly gave Tiki a hug and tried to move away so that no one would see her eyes filling with tears, but Meghan and Elizabeth, who were working on their projects at the same table as Tiki, saw Mrs. Dorn's emotions on full display.

"You're a good teacher, Mrs. D," Meghan whispered to her art teacher.

Her voice cracking, Mrs. Dorn responded, "Thank you, Meghan. And you're a special young lady too" as she dabbed her eyes with a tissue.

"Mrs. Dorn," asked Elizabeth, "would you mind if I inscribed a dedication to the pope on my project?"

"No, not at all, Elizabeth," Mrs. Dorn replied, finally collecting herself. "I know how important he was to you and your family."

"And don't worry," Elizabeth said, with some assertiveness and sarcasm. "I won't pray to this relic or worship it either!" Mrs. Dorn had listened to Elizabeth vent and share her anger and hurt about her second-hour experience in religion class.

"Elizabeth, I'm sure Pastor Andrews did not intentionally set out to embarrass or hurt you in any way. You need to go talk to him and let him know how you feel," Mrs. Dorn said plainly. "I think he would really respect you if you went to talk to him about your hurt. That's what the Bible teaches: if you have a problem with someone, you should go to them one-on-one to rectify the situation." Privately, however, Mrs. Dorn worried that Pastor Andrews might get defensive if questioned by a Catholic student regarding his demeanor and theological acumen. Moreover, she knew of Pastor Andrews's passion for all things Lutheran.

"I get it, Mrs. Dorn," said Elizabeth. "This is a Lutheran school, and he's a Lutheran pastor. He just made me so mad!"

"Well," said Mrs. Dorn, "the Bible teaches that the Holy Spirit will give you the right words. And our school's mission is all about building you up in faith so that you can live and serve confidently, knowing Jesus will be right by your side. Just go talk to him, Elizabeth, and let me know how it goes." Before Mrs. Dorn moved on to the next table to help other students, she looked at Elizabeth's project. "By the way, this is one of your best pieces of work this year." Elizabeth had sculpted a miniature model of Christ Community Lutheran School with a large papal tiara on the roof inscribed with CCLS's mission statement: "Preparing Christian leaders for a life of service and significance."

After class dismissed, Tiki quickly ran up to Mrs. Dorn. "Mrs. Dorn," she whispered. "When my parents come from China next week, please don't tell them about this project. They will not like it. They will not come back; they will leave me here for good."

Fifth Hour

Elizabeth found Pastor Andrews working at his desk during his prep hour, which also happened to be her study hall period. Elizabeth had already developed into a precocious young lady of deep conviction. Almost every night, she and her parents talked about religion and the differences between Lutheran and Catholic beliefs. Ironically, attending a Lutheran school helped her learn more about their own Catholic faith.

Determined to speak her mind, Elizabeth's legs shook as she confronted her theology teacher. "Pastor Andrews, I don't like how you talked about us Catholics today in class," she blurted without a greeting. "The pope is, or was, a really special person to us, but you don't seem to care about that. Everyone laughed at us. And you wouldn't even pray for us! That really hurt." Elizabeth's voice trailed off and cracked as tears welled up in her eyes. Surprised and impressed by this eighth grader's courage, Pastor Andrews rose, walked around his desk, and sat in a student's chair. "Would you sit down with me, Elizabeth?" he pointed to another chair close to him. "Please."

After asking for Elizabeth to explain how he had been insensitive, he listened to her pour out her hurt and anger, once again, as she gave a play-by-play of the beginning of second hour. After listening intently to her without interrupting, Pastor Andrews completely stunned Elizabeth with an apology—for being rude, insensitive, not honoring the prayer request to lift up the families grieving about the pope's passing, for not stopping the other students from ridiculing her Catholic faith, and for putting the three Catholic students on the spot. "Elizabeth, I do believe we Lutherans interpret Scripture properly," he did tell her. "That's why I'm Lutheran. So you have to know I'm going to teach God's Word in all its truth and purity—this is a Lutheran school, after all." He paused and then added, "But the last thing I want to do is give the impression that we Lutherans are insensitive or heartless. Our Savior, after all, is a sensitive Savior."

"Pastor Andrews, I like it here at CCLS," Elizabeth insisted, relieved that he had not made her feel lesser in any way. "My father always says, 'You have to stand for something or you'll fall for anything.' So even if we disagree on some things, I get what you are saying. And you're a lot like my papa, except not Catholic, I guess." Elizabeth chuckled at herself. The two chatted for a few more minutes before Elizabeth asked for a pass back to study hall.

As she started to walk toward the door, Elizabeth turned back. "Pastor, do you believe other Christians—not just Lutherans—will go to heaven?" She paused, and before he could answer she asked one more question: "Do you think I'm going to heaven?"

"Anyone who knows and believes in Jesus Christ as their Lord and Savior will be in heaven, Elizabeth," Pastor Andrews said firmly. "This isn't what I think. This is what God's Word clearly teaches. So yes, if you believe in Jesus Christ as your Lord and Savior, Elizabeth, you and I will have a lot of time in heaven to have many more great conversations." Elizabeth smiled.

"Thank you again for coming in to talk to me, Elizabeth," Pastor Andrews said as she walked toward the door. "I know it took a lot of courage for you to come in here. I'm a sinful human being too—chief of sinners, actually. I make mistakes. So thank you for forgiving me."

Elizabeth had never seen this side of Pastor Andrews before—humble, contrite, even kind. "I do, and thanks for listening. If you couldn't tell, I was scared to death to talk to you, but it wasn't so bad. See you tomorrow."

Sixth Hour

"So what did he say?" Meghan asked Elizabeth as they settled into math class.

"Actually, it was good. He apologized and was even kind of nice." Elizabeth never would have thought that the conversation with Pastor Andrews could go so well.

"Really?" Meghan exclaimed.

"Really. He even prayed the rosary with me."

"What?!"

"Shhhh. I'm just kidding!"

Seventh Hour

After classes had ended for the day, Mrs. Kristin Schwartz, Mrs. Sandra Schlicting, Mrs. Laura Dorn, and Pastor Andrews found themselves sitting next to one another for the afternoon meeting about to commence. Pastor Andrews thanked Laura for encouraging Elizabeth to visit him. "The guy whom I replaced did not use Lutheran materials or books in religion class; instead, he told his students that he was 'just a New Testament guy'—as if God didn't write the Old Testament—and he pushed contemporary guitar worship junk as if it were the cure for cancer," he explained. "He even said living a life of worship is just as important as receiving God's grace in divine worship." He paused. "But maybe I've been so concerned about being different from him and overzealous in showing my Lutheranism that I've been overcompensating a bit, at least in my demeanor and approach."

"Not at all, Pastor," Mrs. Schlicting interjected. "That's why we made the change to get a pastor teaching every day in our day school. The other guy was not properly trained for the job. So don't you go apologizing for anything, Pastor. Let's be who we are—Lutherans!"

"I know if we turn people off or turn them away, we can't teach them God's Word in all of its truth and purity," Mrs. Dorn asserted. "I believe that's the Lutheran way too—teaching God's Word to all of God's children."

"I just love teaching at CCLS," Mrs. Schwartz added. "We've really got it good here, don't we?"

"We've got it good here, and most importantly," Pastor Andrews affirmed, "we've got God here."

Reflection and Discussion

Schools may often feel a tension or challenge in being distinctively Lutheran while also being welcoming to students and families of various other denominations (to say nothing of students and families who come from agnostic or atheistic backgrounds). Read the following Scripture passages as a group or in pairs, and discuss how they apply to this chapter: Hebrews 4:12; James 3:1; 2 Timothy 2:15; Colossians 3:16; Romans 10:17; Hebrews 13:7; 2 Timothy 3:16–17.

1. After reading the Scripture passages and reflecting on the fictionalized story, what can you and your school do to handle or grapple with this tension or challenge?
2. Compare and contrast the different approaches that Ms. Schwartz and Pastor Andrews took with Meghan, Elizabeth, and Nicholas in first and second hour. What would you have done in their context? What lessons can be learned from these interactions?
3. What do you think about Mrs. Schlicting's interactions with Hannah and Ashley during third hour? What did she do well or not so well? What would you have done differently?
4. While the theological differences between different Christian denominations are significant, so are the differences between atheists and Christians. How did Mrs. Dorn handle the situation with Tiki and with Elizabeth? Explain.
5. How did Pastor Andrews handle the situation with Elizabeth in fifth hour? What lessons can be drawn from their conversation?

CHAPTER 19

A NEW TEACHER AND THE LEAGUE OF EXTRAORDINARY GAME MASTERS

BY BERNARD BULL

Craig Swanson was not your ordinary teacher. He taught sixth-grade science, but he thought of himself as more of a game master. As he liked to describe it, he got paid to blow things up, design games, set up fun experiments, and watch kids learn. He prided himself on not being your typical teacher.

When Craig went to middle school years before, he hated school. Science was his least favorite class because a bully kicked his chair and back almost every day while the teacher droned on at the front of the class, displaying what seemed like an eternal series of text-filled PowerPoint slides. As Craig described it, there was no wonder in that classroom.

Craig loved science; he hated science class. He received his first chemistry set for Christmas at age 10 and proceeded to beg for every possible science kit, educational game, or gadget for all subsequent birthdays and holidays. The contrast between what he experienced in middle school science class and what he loved about science at home set the path for his future. While sitting in the back of a middle school classroom, trying his best to stay awake, Craig made the decision that he would grow up to be a completely different type of science teacher. He was going to be fun, engaging, wacky, and even a little weird. He dreamed of growing his hair out to look like one of those old photos of Einstein in which he looks like he just stuck his finger in an electric socket.

Fast-forward ten years, and Craig was a recent college graduate and a first-year middle school science teacher with mad-scientist flair. Every day, he made it a personal mission to tap into the curiosity of his students, to invite them into the wonders of the natural world and the joys of game-based, quest-based, experiential, and curiosity-driven learning. Students arrived in class with some sort of challenge or clue on the board. The necessary materials were set out, often with props and decorations tied to the theme for the day. Every day in this class culminated with some sort of interesting science experiment, quest, or game, followed by a group debriefing about what they experienced and learned from it.

Craig's class could not be more different than what he had experienced as a kid. Nobody sat bored in his class. In fact, students hardly ever even sat in desks. They were on the floor, outdoors, or gathered in a huddle around some sort of puzzle or experiment. They were thinking, moving, collaborating, laughing, problem-solving, experimenting, and theorizing.

This was not just some special event. It was a normal day in his classroom. He approached each day with the energy, passion, and attention to detail that you might expect of a wedding planner. Each detail mattered. Every student mattered. Each game, experiment, or simulation was designed and carefully prepared, and you could see the pride and playful smirk on Craig's face as he watched students walk into class and get drawn into the activities for the day. For some days, it was a single-class challenge. At other times, the challenge or experiment extended over days or even a week.

One morning, Craig arrived early to get his class set up for a new challenge. He turned on the classroom lights and saw a large red box sitting on the floor in the middle of the room with a message next to it: "Are you ready for a challenge, Mr. Swanson? Read the riddle on the back, and let the games begin!" The box had three padlocks on it.

Craig grinned in delight. His students had shifted from game players to game makers. For the next forty-five minutes, Craig struggled from riddle to riddle, taking him outside, back into the classroom, and then outside again. Each riddle led to the next, and each challenge tied into this wonderfully creative story. In the story, Craig was an undercover spy disguised as a middle school science teacher, and he only had an hour to solve the riddles and save the planet.

He figured out the final clue and removed the last lock from the box, saved the world, and raised his arms in that classic epic-win pose of victory. He opened it to find a box full of thank-you letters from his students. Each one, of course, required a cipher to decode. Looking at the clock, he had just thirty minutes before the first class started that day, so he set the box aside for some evening fun and finished preparations for the day.

As students arrived one by one, they each entered the room with a look of clever pride, excited to see the teacher's reaction. Craig pretended like it was just an ordinary day, but once everybody was there, he gathered them in a circle on the floor. He told them the story of his morning adventure, the strange box that he found in the room, and the series of clever riddles that clearly took a deep knowledge of science to create. After thanking them for providing him with such a wonderful gift, he shifted the conversation back to the students.

Craig loved to debrief the learning experiences with the students, and this situation was no different. He asked them about the process of designing the game. He asked about what worked well and what was challenging for them. He asked about how they collaborated in the design. Then he invited them to consider what they learned through the process of designing such a "learning experience."

The students were excited to tell their stories. It turns out that this design took them almost two weeks of researching, planning, meeting, and experimenting. They tested the riddles on one another, gathered feedback, and revised. They even reached out to a couple of professional game designers on the internet to get input on their project. Craig listened with astonishment. He knew they were an engaged and curious group, but he had no idea that they were capable of such work.

He wondered what would happen if he invited the students to join in the design of the games, experiments, and adventures in the class more consistently. He shared this musing with the class, and a group of more than half of the students volunteered to join what they decided to call "The League of Extraordinary Game Masters." Each day after school, this group met to plan and map out games and experiments for the rest of the school year. They learned to align the experiences with mandated standards. They learned how to embed assessments; they discovered various ways to check for student understanding of key ideas. They learned about how to design rich learning experiences that not only engaged students but also truly helped students learn. Along the way, they also learned about science while discovering important lessons about how to learn.

Craig loved surprising students with daily challenges, immersive games, and engaging experiments. Yet it didn't take long for him to see the incredible power of inviting students to be designers of their own experiences. As the semester continued, a growing number of students volunteered to join the League of Extraordinary Game Masters. By the end of the year, the students designed and managed almost every game and experiment, and student learning was as strong as ever.

Reflection and Discussion

As with some of the other tales in this book, this one sounds almost too good to be true. In fact, it probably is too good to be true. In the real world of our schools and classrooms, few things typically work out quite as smoothly as what you just read. Nonetheless, following are some questions for your reflection and consideration; ultimately, let them prompt your thinking about your own practice.

1. What is your experience with using challenges and games in the classroom?
2. As you think about past or possible future uses of games in the classroom, what most interests you? What are the roadblocks? As you consider roadblocks, what are some possible ways through each of them?
3. As with some of the other stories in this book, the role of students comes up. While designing games for students can be effective, see if you can come up with a couple ideas on how you could invite students to design learning games for themselves and their classmates.
4. Educational game design, like most things, is a skill set that takes time to develop. Consider finding a few articles, books, or other resources that could deepen your understanding. However, ultimately game design is best learned by doing it. Look at your curriculum for the year. Can you identity two or three units that might lend themselves to the use or design of an educational game?

THE TECHNOPHILE TEACHER AND THE ACTION RESEARCH TRANSFORMATION

BY BERNARD BULL

Cassie was a fifth-grade teacher who loved technology. She liked her students and teaching too, but she occupied almost all of her free time exploring new educational technologies and brainstorming ways to integrate these technologies in her classroom. She prided herself on being on the cutting edge, aware of every new app or technological tool with a possible educational application. At the end-of-year evaluations, she always made her professional goals for the upcoming year about technology. When interactive whiteboards first came out, she was the first to get one in her class. When one-to-one technology programs were just an idea for most schools, she was the one who lobbied to run a pilot with her students. When Google Apps became widely available, she was the first to go through the training and become a trainer for others.

Each day, she worked to impress her students with a new app, online tool, or piece of hardware. It didn't matter what she was teaching; Cassie could find a way to integrate technology, and she did it consistently. Sometimes this integration enhanced the lesson. Sometimes it was hard to tell how the use of technology would actually be an improvement on the low-tech solutions. Nevertheless, for Cassie, the technology option always beat out the traditional method.

When other teachers questioned a particular use of technology or didn't share Cassie's approach, she tried to be nice about it, but inside she thought they were out of touch and on the path to obsolescence. The future of education was a technological one, and Cassie intended to be part of that future. Yet if you asked her to explain her thinking about why she used a given technological tie-in for a lesson, she didn't provide much of an answer beyond explaining that this was new and promising technology. In fact, she became visibly frustrated, even angry, when people questioned her use of technology.

You could always expect that her reply to those who asked about the benefit or value would include words such as *exciting*, *innovative*, *hot*, *cutting edge*, *entrepreneurial*, *future-ready*, *engaging*, and *fun*. It was less common for her to cite research that informed her decisions or to give any answer that went beyond keeping the kids' attention through the use of something new. For Cassie, integrating technology was the goal. Good and future-oriented teachers integrated new technologies. Such teachers knew the latest buzzwords and tools, and they knew how to use them.

One day, the principal of her school announced a brand-new educational technology program. She had heard rumors that this initiative was coming, so she was the first to the faculty meeting, sitting at a table near the front, anxious for the news and ready to sign up for whatever pilot or experiment the principal was about to launch. When the principal started talking, her excitement grew even more. It turned out that an anonymous donor created an educational technology fund for the school, thirty thousand dollars all dedicated to support educational technology experiments in the classroom. Any teacher could submit a proposal and it would get reviewed based upon a set of criteria set up by the donor. However, this money came with a catch.

A teacher submitting a proposal could receive up to five thousand dollars at a time for any educational technology program, but the proposal had to meet strict requirements. First, any proposal had to start with a problem statement that answered the question, "What is the educational problem you want to solve or the educational opportunity that you want to pursue?" As the principal explained, simply wanting to try out new technology wouldn't suffice. Any innovation must start with a focus on the students and their educational needs.

Second, the proposal had to include a small review of current research or literature about how others have sought to solve that problem or pursue that educational opportunity. In other words, you had to prove that you did your homework, that you explored what was working and not working in other places. It wasn't enough to suggest a new idea.

Third, teachers submitting a proposal would have to engage the students in researching the problem or opportunity and exploring possible solutions. A teacher's lone-ranger idea was not enough. This had to be a team effort with the learners.

Fourth, there had to be a plan on what would be done to solve the problem or pursue the opportunity, again drawing input and insights from the students. The more the students were involved, the better. Each part of the plan needed to be drawn from insights in the literature review.

The last two requirements involved feedback and results. The fifth requirement of the proposal called for a plan to monitor the plan once it was implemented. How would the teachers and students assess and analyze the plan along the way? The last requirement involved a post-project assessment that reflected on what worked and what did not, potential next steps, and lessons learned along the way. A public presentation of these findings would be required within twelve months of receiving any funding, and this, too, should involve significant student engagement.

Cassie listened intently to the criteria for the project. She remained excited about the prospect of this money for new technology, but she was not nearly as excited after listening to all the expectations. It seemed like a ton of unnecessary work to her. She wondered why the donor would add so many rules, noting that this was sure to prevent teachers from taking advantage of it. While she didn't tell anyone else, she was intimidated by such expectations. Not only had she never done a literature review before, but she also didn't have experience engaging students in such a project. As much as Cassie talked about collaboration in her class because it was a valued word in the educational technology community, she preferred to do things on her own. You can get things done faster and better without having to coordinate and build consensus in a team, she reasoned to herself. This attitude also stemmed from past experiences working with teams of faculty members on projects on which one or two people ended up doing all the work. For these and many other reasons, Cassie left the room disappointed, but she was still committed to doing what it took to get some of this new funding.

Being a twenty-first-century educator, she spent the entire evening browsing the web, looking up more about some of the words and phrases mentioned by the principal. One of the phrases she noted on her electronic tablet during the principal's announcement was "action research," so she started there. Seeing herself as more of a visual and auditory learner (some buzzwords that had stuck with her from her earliest days in teaching), she focused on searches on Pinterest and YouTube. She was most intrigued by the YouTube videos of teachers who shared their stories of conducting "action research" and how it transformed their classes in fascinating ways. She even found a few stories in which the teachers engaged the students in the process. With each new video, Cassie's confidence grew, and she started to come around to see the potential wisdom in making this a requirement of getting the funding.

Inspired by these stories, Cassie decided to invite a group of her students to an after-school meeting later in the week to explore the possibilities. This was far outside of her comfort zone. She knew and loved technology, but this sort of analytical and research-based approach in education was completely new. With no small measure of self-doubt, uncertainty, and excitement, she hosted the meeting with the students. Explaining the new program as best as she could, Cassie invited the students to share potential educational problems. She intentionally selected a diverse group of students, especially in terms of their academic performance.

Once the conversation started, Cassie's nerves subsided as she immersed herself in listening to the fascinating stories and perspectives. She talked to her students often, but she had never before engaged them in this sort of conversation about teaching and learning. From the straight-A student in the group to the one who seemed to sleep through most classes, this group contributed rich insights.

After an hour, the group started to notice a pattern in their concerns and comments. They noticed that the course, which most of them enjoyed, too often seemed like just another required middle school course. They didn't think about it in terms of what they could learn from it that had relevance for their current and future lives or for their personal goals. They decided to focus their work on coming up with a way to make sure that every student found meaning and relevance in everything studied in the class. They didn't know how to accomplish this yet, but they were determined to figure it out.

That is exactly what they did. The group met three times a week for the next two months. They framed the problem, garnering input from other classmates. They started conducting research, including inviting some of the leading researchers on the topic to join them via FaceTime, Skype, or Google Hangouts. In the end, Cassie and this small group of students put together an impressive proposal that resulted in a five-thousand-dollar grant. Far from a simple request to buy technology, this proposal included a collection of technological applications, new learning activities, and a new way of approaching lessons in the class. For the rest of the year, Cassie and her new research team implemented the plan, monitored its progress, and excitedly shared their findings at a regional educational conference, where dozens of teachers decided to try out this plan in their classes as well.

Reflection and Discussion

1. During the Reformation, Martin Luther utilized the cutting-edge technology of his time, the printing press, to spread the message of the Gospel in new and culture-changing ways. As Christian teachers who want to utilize the most effective means possible to teach and share the love of Jesus, how do you make decisions about what technology to use, when, and how?
2. What role does research play in making plans and decisions about technology or teaching and learning in your classroom (in your school as well)?
3. Notice how the focus for Cassie shifted from technology to teaching and learning. Where is the focus in your classroom and in your school?
4. What role do students play in researching and analyzing possibilities in your classroom and school?
5. Revisit the five requirements of a proposal for the grant in this story. Identity a challenge or opportunity in your school or classroom. Try using those five elements to sketch out a brief plan for how you might go about addressing that challenge or pursuing that opportunity. Better yet, consider inviting a small group of people to brainstorm and do the work with you.